1998

Alexander the Great

IN THE SAME SERIES

General Editors: Eric J. Evans and P. D. King

LANCASTER PAMPHLETS

Alexander the Great

Richard Stoneman

London and New York

First published 1997
by Routledge
11 New Fetter Lane, London EC4P 4EE

Simultaneously published in the USA and Canada
by Routledge
29 West 35th Street, New York, NY 10001
© 1997 Richard Stoneman

Typeset in Bembo by
Ponting–Green Publishing Services, Chesham, Buckinghamshire
Printed and bound in Great Britain by
Clays Ltd, St. Ives PLC

British Library Cataloguing in Publication Data
A catalogue record for this book is available from
the British Library

Library of Congress Cataloguing in Publication Data
Stoneman, Richard
Alexander the Great / Richard Stoneman
p. cm. – (Lancaster pamphlets)
Includes bibliographical references.
1. Alexander, the Great, 356–323 B.C.
2. Generals – Greece – Biography
3. Greece – Kings and rulers – Biography
4. Greece – History – Macedonian Expansion, 359–323 B.C.
I. Title II. Series.
DF234.S76   1997
938'.07'092–dc21   97–7028

ISBN 0–415–15050–7

Contents

Foreword

Lancaster Pamphlets offer concise and up-to-date accounts of major historical topics, primarily for the help of students preparing for Advanced Level examinations, though they should also be of value to those pursuing introductory courses in universities and other institutions of higher education. Without being all-embracing, their aims are to bring some of the central themes or problems confronting students and teachers into sharper focus than the textbook writer can hope to do; to provide the reader with some of the results of recent research which the textbook may not embody; and to stimulate thought about the whole interpretation of the topic under discussion.

Preface

There are many books on Alexander the Great, and the aim of this one is modest: to introduce students to the outlines of his career and the main problems of the sources, and to provide some orientation for further study of Alexander. I have emphasised perhaps more than is usual the significance of Alexander's impact on the world that followed him, in legend and philosophy as well as in political practice. More than most historical figures, Alexander is one whose career resonates today, not least in contemporary Greece and its Balkan neighbours, where his fame still serves ideological purposes.

I am grateful to the series editors for their invitation to contribute to this series, and their comments on the typescript; also to David Shotter for his careful criticisms of style and presentation. Michael Whitby read the whole text with great attention and is responsible for very many improvements. The errors that remain are my own.

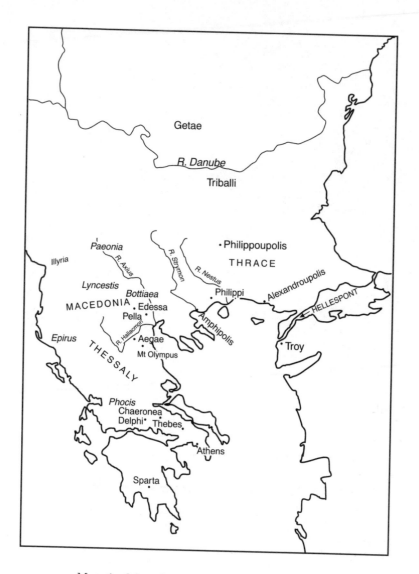

Map 1: Macedonia and neighbouring lands

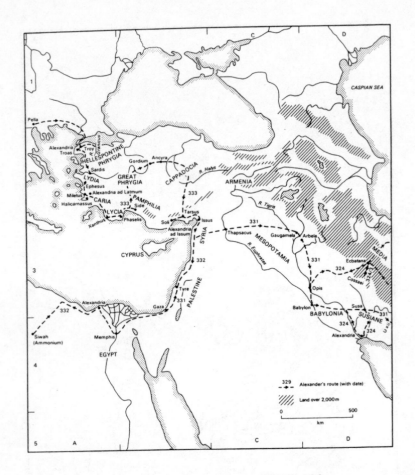

Map 2: Alexander's campaigns 334–323 BC

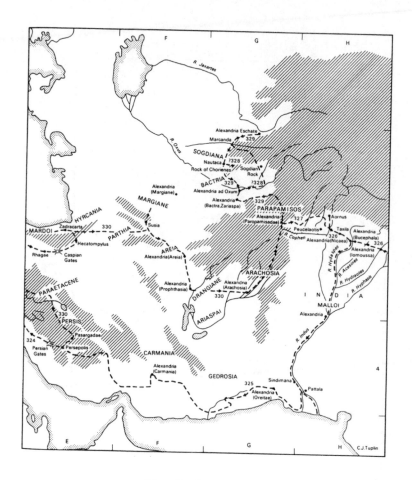

Map 2: (continued)

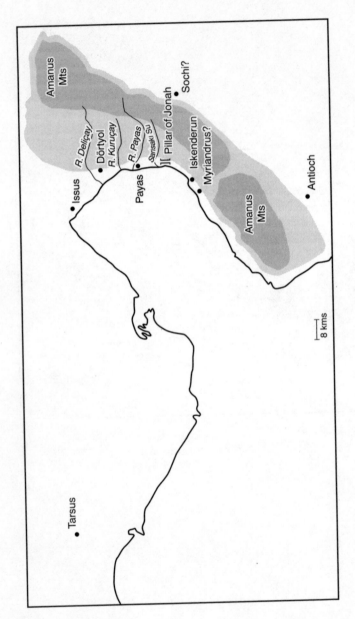

Map 3: Environs of Issus

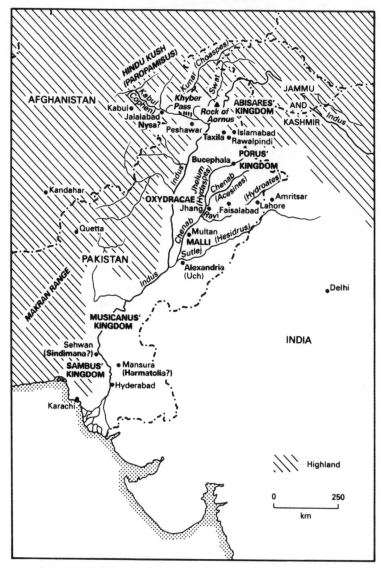

Map 4: Pakistan, showing sites visited by Alexander

Genealogy

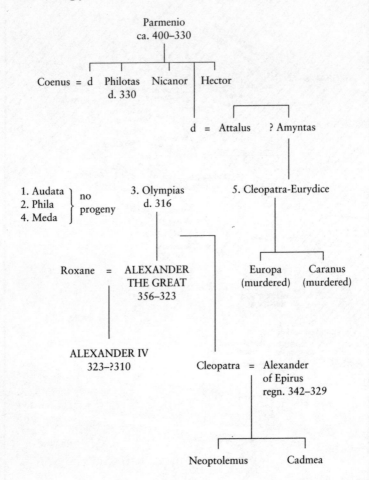

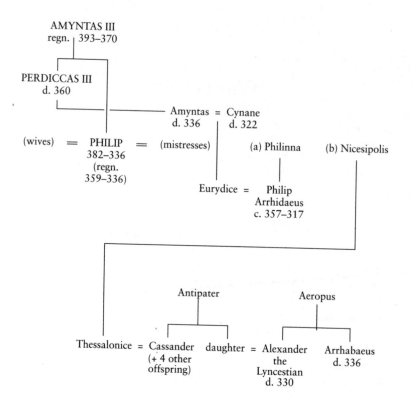

Chronology

331, Oct 1	Battle of Gaugamela
331–330, winter	Macedonian army at Persepolis
330, spring	Move to Ecbatana
330, summer	Death of Darius. Harpalus' return to Babylon
330, autumn	'Conspiracy of Philotas' discovered at Phrada. Execution of Philotas and his father Parmenio
329, spring	Crossing of Hindu Kush; capture of Bessus
329–328	Alexander at Maracanda; foundation of Alexandria-the-furthest; campaigns in Sogdia (presumably)
328, autumn	Alexander murders Clitus
328–327, winter	Suppression of Spitamenes
327, spring	Conquest of Sogdian Rock; marriage of Alexander and Roxane
327–early 326	Reorganisation of army. Embassies from Taxiles. Visit to Nysa
326, spring	Arrival in Taxila. Battle on the Hydaspes. Twelve altars constructed on the Hyphasis
326, Nov – spring 325	Voyage down the Indus. Siege of town of the Malli
325, summer	Arrival at Pattala
325, Sept	Alexander begins march across Gedrosian Desert. Nearchus embarks in fleet for Persian Gulf
325, autumn	Arrival in Carmania
324, Feb	Marriages at Susa
324, July	Mutiny at Opis. Exiles Decree
324, Oct	Death of Hephaestion at Ecbatana. Murder of Harpalus (about now)
323, spring	Alexander arrives in Babylon
323, June 10	Death of Alexander
323, Aug	Birth of Alexander IV. Lamian War
321	Death of Craterus and Perdiccas
317, Sept	Murder of Philip III by Olympias
316	Execution of Olympias

Abbreviations

App. *Syr.*: Appian, *Syrian History*
Arr. *Anab.*: Arrian, *Anabasis* (Expedition of Alexander)
Curt.: Quintus Curtius Rufus, *Historia Alexandri*
Diod. Sic.: Diodorus Siculus
FGrHist: *Fragmente der griechischen Historiker*, ed. F. Jacoby
(citations give number of author, F for 'fragment', followed by
number of fragment)
Josephus, *AJ*: Josephus, *Antiquities of the Jews*
Just.: Justin, *Epitome* (of Trogus)
Pliny *NH*: Pliny, *Naturalis Historia*
Plut. *Alex.*: Plutarch, *Life of Alexander*
Plut. *de fort. Alex.*: Plutarch, *de fortuna Alexandri* (on Alex-
ander's Fortune)
Seneca, *NQ*: Seneca, *Natural Questions*
Strabo: Strabo, *Geography*

AJAH: *American Journal of Ancient History*
CQ: *Classical Quarterly*
Entretiens Hardt: *Entretiens de la Fondation Hardt*
JHS: *Journal of Hellenic Studies*
PACA: Proceedings of the African Classical Association
S.B. Akad. Berlin: *Sitzungsberichte der Akademie der Wissen-
schaften zu Berlin*
TAPA: Transactions of the American Philological Association

1

Introduction: the sources

Alexander the Great was born in summer 356 BC and died thirty-three years later in the month Daisios (June) 323 BC. He was born the son of Philip, the king of Macedon, a fertile and predominantly pastoral region lying north of classical Greece; he died in Babylon, the son – according to some authors, and perhaps his own belief – of the god Zeus Ammon, and ruler of most of the known world lying to the east and south of Greece. In a reign of thirteen years, eleven of them spent away from his country and his capital, campaigning in hitherto unexplored regions, he created a new world which, though impermanent politically, represented a radical cultural change in the Near East. Quickly attaining mastery of the fragmented city-states of classical Greece, and imbued with a warm admiration of Greek culture, he carried, almost by accident, the Greek language and civilisation to the regions he traversed. He conquered the Persian Empire, which included not only the Iranian heartlands but also all the Semitic-speaking regions between the Zagros Mountains and the Mediterranean Sea, and Asia Minor with its mixed population of Greeks, Lycians, Carians and numerous other peoples.

The world he left behind him, split as it quickly was between several successor-kings, retained the Greek language as its medium of communication and Greek culture as its frame of reference. The Persian Empire had used Aramaic as its lingua franca, but Greek now spread over a far wider area than that where Aramaic had been spoken. And Greek language and culture – Hellenism – provided the medium for the establishment of greater, more permanent subsequent dominions, first among them the Roman Empire. The spread of Christianity could hardly be imagined without the conquests of Alexander the Great. The Hellenistic world lasted, according to some perspectives, to the fall of Byzantium in AD 1453, and has even been said to have ended only with the Treaty of Rome in AD 1956.

To describe these achievements is not to aver that they were part of Alexander's intention. When, as a young, ambitious and romantic youth with a genius for military strategy and tactics, he embarked on the conquest of the Persian Empire, he may have had no more in mind than the setting to rights of the perceived age-old wrong inflicted by the Persians on the Greeks. World conquest may have come along as an afterthought. As with all individuals in the ancient world, we have hopelessly inadequate information from which to assess Alexander's own interests, ideals, hopes and motivations. It has been said that the main problem in Alexander studies is the problem of the sources (Badian 1976, 297; Hammond 1983, 166). Because of the difficulties in assessing the surviving sources, modern interpretations vary widely (Robinson 1953, 1; see the discussion in Chapter 1).

Alexander left no official writings of his own (though some of the letters ascribed to him may be genuine). Nor do we have more than fragments from the contemporary writers who described his career. And these writers were numerous. His expedition was accompanied by a retinue of intellectuals, including the bematists (who noted the stages of the march day by day), an official historian (Callisthenes), a couple of philosophers (Onesicritus and Anaxarchus), as well as scientists to study the geography, ethnography and fauna of the regions he passed through.

These works were followed by histories written shortly after Alexander's death by those who accompanied him. All these are lost and are known to us only through their use by the authors of full-length accounts dating from the first century BC and later. As might be expected, these works reflect widely different moral viewpoints, from admiration of the great commander to disapprobation of the tyrant corrupted by Fortune. It is a hard task to penetrate the accreted opinions to a clear view of the mental world of Alexander – and probably impossible. His career thus raises in a particularly acute form the issue of source-criticism, and anyone who sets out to study Alexander must be aware of the routes and channels by which our information has reached us. The remainder of this introduction will therefore concentrate on a sketch of the main sources of information about Alexander and the judgements and prejudices they impose on the material.

The bematists need little attention; their fragments are few and their job was to record the mundane details of the march. The works were probably written up after Alexander's death. More curious is the case of the Royal Diaries (*Ephemerides*), which *prima facie* might seem very good first-hand evidence for Alexander's career; however, only one long passage is known from them, which deals with Alexander's last days, and it is possible that they covered no more than the last few months of Alexander's life. Their genuineness has been frequently im-pugned, and will be discussed in Chapter 7 where they have a bearing on the narrative. Only Hammond accepts them as a genuine source lying behind Ptolemy and thence Arrian. Alex-ander's Will is a plain later forgery; and the 'Last Plans' reported by Diodorus have also been the subject of considerable scepti-cism, though current opinion seems to favour their genuineness (again, see the discussion in Chapter 7).

Of those who accompanied Alexander's expedition it is worth mentioning Chares of Mytilene, his chamberlain, author of 'Stories of Alexander', and some other anecdotal authors – Medeius of Larissa, Polyclitus of Larissa, and Ephippus of Olynthus. Of greater importance is Callisthenes of Olynthus, the nephew of Aristotle, taken along in a journalistic capacity to write up the history of the expedition as it proceeded. What is left of it evinces a highly laudatory approach to Alexander. However, Callisthenes, like many of the Greeks, disapproved strongly of the orientalising ways Alexander adopted after the final defeat and death of the Persian king Darius; he was implicated in the Conspiracy of the Pages (spring 327) and executed. The last attested event covered by his history is the battle of Gaugamela, though it may have run to 328. His name

3

became attached to the *Alexander Romance* for reasons that are hard to fathom.

Full histories of the expedition were also written by Onesicritus of Astypalaea, a Cynic philosopher who accompanied the expedition and interviewed the Indian ascetics at Taxila on Alexander's behalf; by Nearchus, who commanded the fleet which sailed down the Indus and back to Babylon; and by two authors of great importance for the later tradition: Aristobulus, the technical expert, and Ptolemy, later king of Egypt. Finally there is Cleitarchus, whose relation to Ptolemy and Aristobulus is uncertain: his work, in twelve books, was probably written before the end of the fourth century, but there has been some dispute as to whether he accompanied the expedition or not. The balance of probability seems to be that he was with Alexander in Babylon, if not earlier in the expedition.

Cleitarchus is of great importance as the ultimate source of the Vulgate tradition on Alexander the Great, represented by Diodorus, Curtius and Justin. Cleitarchus had a propensity to record whatever was wonderful, a charge not inapplicable to other early historians, too: a good example is his account of Alexander's meeting and sexual liaison with the queen of the Amazons, the description of which prompted the later king Lysimachus (who accompanied Alexander) to remark, 'Where was I at the time?' Cleitarchus is the only author – as far as we can trace the origin of the statements in the extant historians – to make Alexander the son of the god Ammon. In general he seeks to glorify Alexander, and also often exaggerates the role of Ptolemy (for reasons that are not clear, though if he was writing in Ptolemy's Alexandria we might see an explanation there).

The fondness for the wonderful exhibited by Cleitarchus infected the *Alexander Romance* to a very marked degree. This is a fantastic historical novel, probably dating from a generation or two after Alexander's death. It is of no use as history, though it does occasionally support conclusions drawn from the other historians. Many of the events in the *Romance* are 'actings-out' of desires expressed by Alexander in the Vulgate historians, such as his conquest of Ethiopia or his reaching the end of the world. But the *Romance* cannot be attached to the Cleitarchan tradition: it contains too much unique material. The core of the *Romance* is a 'foundation history' of the city of Alexandria, but it also exhibits a strong moral tone in respect of the desire the fictional Alexander exhibits for immortality.

The so-called Vulgate tradition comprises several full length histories of Alexander's reign, all of which made use of a selection of these now lost-writers, but all of which were written several centuries later. These are the relevant portions of the universal history by Diodorus of Sicily known as the *Bibliotheca* ('Library'); the *History of Alexander* by Quintus Curtius Rufus (probably first century AD); and the *Histories of Philip* by Pompeius Trogus (first century BC) preserved for us only in an abridged version ('epitome') by Justin (probably before AD 230). Though we are thus plentifully supplied with detail about events (which is not often in radical conflict), interpretation is at least second-hand.

Other writers lying behind the Vulgate, who are used only by Diodorus, include the obscure Diyllus, who provided a narrative framework, and Ephippus, who wrote on the death of Alexander and of Philip. For the period following Alexander's death Diodorus drew on Hieronymus of Cardia.

The alternative to the Vulgate is represented by Arrian (*c.* AD 86–160), a philosopher, senator and military man who wrote in Greek in the reign of Hadrian (117–38). His longest work was his seventeen-book history of the Parthian campaigns of Trajan, an emperor much obsessed with eastern conquest and the example of Alexander. In his *Anabasis of Alexander*, Arrian writes admiringly but not uncritically of Alexander, and rejects all the fabulous elements that have infected the other writers. He explicitly states that he has taken as his main authorities Aristobulus and Ptolemy, giving as his reason for preference for the latter the fact that 'as a king, it would be unseemly for him to lie'. We owe to Arrian the identification of the driving feature of Alexander's personality: his *pothos* or 'desire', his constant yearning to go further, which does seem to explain many of his actions. Arrian is generally regarded as the most reliable basis for the construction of a narrative of Alexander's career; but it must be emphasised that his work, as much as any of the other extant works, is a secondary one.

The final source to which recourse may be had is the *Life of Alexander* written as part of his series of Parallel Lives by Plutarch (about AD 50–120). Plutarch had access to what he describes as an extensive body of correspondence by Alexander himself, some of which may have been genuine; he made plentiful use of this as his main aim was to construct a moral portrait of Alexander rather than a consecutive history. Revealing anecdote is privileged over meticulous narrative. The *Life* contains much valuable material, and considerably deepens the portrait in Plutarch's own youthful essays 'On the fortune of Alexander'. These reflect the tradition of composing moralising rhetorical exercises on the theme of Alexander, such as are extant in the works of the Elder and Younger Seneca (first century AD) and the orator Dio Chrysostom (second century, a contemporary of Trajan).

Ancient historians today generally supplement the record of the ancient writers with the findings of archaeology, including the study of inscriptions, sculpture and coins. In Alexander's case such sources are of limited value. His major city foundation, Alexandria in Egypt, is entirely covered by modern Alexandria and cannot be investigated. Many of the other Alexandrias he founded cannot now be located, and those that can – perhaps Ai Khanum, certainly Merv, Herat and Kandahar – are not ready to be explored and perhaps would reveal little in any case. (Some of them may not actually date back as far as Alexander's reign but may be foundations of Seleucus I.) The fact that Tyre is now permanently joined to the mainland by the mole built by Alexander for his six-month siege of the city in 332 is impressive, but not especially revealing. His inscriptions are for the most part simple dedications (like that from the rebuilt temple of Athena at Priene, which is now in the British Museum). A little more can be gained from the study of his coinage (see pp. 56, 68) and from the very numerous sculptural portraits, which convey something of the personality, more of the ambition to godhead; and which established types for the portrayal of Hellenistic rulers for the next two centuries.

Direct evidence for Alexander's career is thus scarce or problematic. What we have is an enormous amount of secondary evidence. The factual and chronological framework can be reconstructed with reasonable consistency: interpretation remains somewhat poorly based, and even on major historical issues such as the guilt or innocence of conspirators against Alexander (Philotas, Callisthenes) no firm conclusion can be reached. But enough is left to leave no doubt that in dealing with Alexander we are dealing with one of very few individuals in history who can truly be said to have changed the world irrevocably. This may go some way to explain the endurance of his name and legend throughout the ages on an almost unparalleled scale.

The names of many modern scholars will occur in these pages in discussion of the important issues on which opinion is divided. It is therefore worth outlining briefly the way in which views of Alexander have developed over the century and a half since modern historical scholarship began. The following summary draws heavily on the indispensable article by Ernst Badian, 'Some recent interpretations of Alexander' (1976).

The first major scholarly treatment of Alexander's career was that of J. G. Droysen (2nd edn 1877), who saw Philip and Alexander as the Bismarcks of their age, uniting the world under Hellenic leadership and acting according to a kind of divine plan to unify the world and infect it with the spirit of the Greek *polis*. This remained the dominant view, with modifications, through the soberer work of Ulrich Wilcken (1922) and W. W. Tarn (1948), whom Badian describes as 'Droysen translated into the King's English'. For Tarn, Alexander could do no wrong; very few blemishes on his unstained and heroic character are admitted, and he is credited with a mission not only to bring Greek culture to the rest of the world but also to blend all mankind in unity and brotherhood.

This view is scarcely less extravagant than the early view of F. Schachermeyr, expressed in his book *Indogermanen und Orient* of 1940, which proposed a Nazi-influenced racial interpretation and saw the 'mixing of cultures' as a dangerous 'Chaos of Blood'. In his later work Schachermeyr repudiated this ideologically driven view, and in his book of 1973, and associated studies, presents Alexander as a 'titanic but flawed' maker of history.

Badian's own work from 1958 onwards represented a decisive swing of the pendulum. Deeply influenced by the spectacle of the Nazis' rise to power and totalitarian rule, Badian interpreted Alexander as a thoroughgoing tyrant, ruthless and cruel. He speaks of Alexander's last years as a 'reign of terror', and presents Alexander as an evil monarch with few redeeming features. In addition, Badian's work has been instrumental in dispelling the idea that Alexander had a Hellenic 'mission', partly by emphasising the continuing dominance of Macedonians, as distinct from Greeks, in his ruling élite, and partly by concentrating on the power-politics of Alexander's career. Perhaps the last representatives of the belief in this mission were Victor Ehrenberg (1938) and Tarn (1948).

To modern tastes such an image of the conqueror is perhaps more naturally acceptable than the earlier attitude of hero-worship, and it has certainly influenced more recent scholars, of whom the doyen is now A. B. Bosworth. Bosworth's work since 1970, while rejecting the more overtly moralistic stance of Badian, has certainly done much to emphasise the negative aspects of Alexander's rule – his failures and irresponsibilities – and the pragmatic and opportunistic decision-making that gained him his successes, rather than any settled policy or 'mission'.

The 'warts-and-all' approach to Alexander was taken up by Peter Green in a biography (1974) which seems positively to revel in the most ghoulish and discreditable stories about Alexander, often from unreliable sources. But the image of the conqueror that emerges from its pages is a plausible one, of a brilliant and ruthless commander who came to believe his own myth. It makes wonderful reading – as does the biography by Robin Lane Fox (1973), which represents something of a return to the heroic model of Alexander. Though far from starry-eyed, this treatment does emphasise the epic scale of Alexander's achievement. The book was savagely reviewed by Badian in the *New York Review of Books* as a work which purveyed all the qualities to be expected of an upper-class, Old Etonian English author. Truly the two interpretations can never meet; but Lane Fox is one of a minuscule number of scholars who have actually covered most of the ground which Alexander trod, and the insights to be gained from this experience, as well as the scholarship that informs every page of the book, make the work one that can not be so dismissed.

Another important contribution of recent years (from 1978) has been the scholarly output of N. G. L. Hammond. Hammond is a scholar second to none in the history of Macedonia and northern Greece; and his two book-length studies of the sources for Alexander (1983 and 1993) are indispensable for serious study, even if their confidence in the possibility of identifying the source of every statement in the historians seems sometimes rather old-fashioned.

This brief survey is of course not complete and does not include many scholars who have made major but more specific or local contributions to Alexander studies. But they represent the names which set the tone of interpretation, and which will appear most frequently in these pages.

2

The Macedonian background

The kingdom of Macedon to which Alexander succeeded in 336 was an oddity in the Greek world. It resembled its southern neighbour Thessaly in being a territorial state rather than being centred on a *polis* or 'city-state' like Athens, Sparta or Thebes; but it was more centralised in its structure even than Thessaly, in that it was ruled by an absolute monarch of a pattern recalling that of the *basileis* of the Homeric poems.

Macedon, under a strong central administration, gradually obtained rule over neighbouring regions and peoples until, by the reign of Philip II (359–36), it controlled the regions of Paeonia to the north and the Lyncestian people to the west. These regions were known as Upper Macedonia. Philip's conquests extended Macedonian territory eastwards as well, beyond the River Strymon to the Nestus (in which area he founded Philippi), and even beyond the Rhodope mountain range of Thrace, where he founded the city of Philippoupolis (Plovdiv). These conquests gave him full control of the gold mines of Thrace and the timber forests of the Strymon region, and enabled the huge growth in power and ambition that characterised his reign and that of his son.

A famous speech which Alexander is said to have made to his troops during the mutiny at Opis in 324 summarises the contemporary perception of these achievements:

When Philip took you over you were nomadic and poor, the majority of you clad in skins and grazing sparse herds on the mountains, putting up a poor fight for them against Illyrians, Triballians and the neighbouring Thracians. He gave you cloaks to wear in place of skins. He brought you down from the mountains to the plains, making you a match in battle for the neighbouring barbarians, trusting for your salvation no longer in the natural strength of places so much as in your own courage. He made you dwellers in cities and graced your lives with good laws and customs.

(Arr. *Anab.* 7.9.2)

He goes on to mention the expansion of trade, the security of mining, and Philip's conquests in Greece.

It has often been considered that Alexander – if the detail of the speech is authentic – overstates the case. There were cities in Macedon before Philip, and there was culture, too, as we shall see. But these sentences reflect the perception of the Greeks further south, that the Macedonians were a rustic, backward – even 'barbarian' – people. The charge of 'barbarism' requires explanation. The term was used by Greeks to describe any people who did not speak Greek – whose language sounded (to them) like 'bar-bar'. Were the Macedonians Greeks?

Scholarly opinion remains divided over the issue, and there is little enough direct evidence to draw on. Against the Greek identity of Macedonians is the Greek prejudice described above, and best-evinced by Demosthenes' invectives against Philip in the course of the latter's conquests; but Demosthenes, seeing himself as a defender of Athenian liberty, had an axe to grind. The other piece of evidence is the complaint made by Alexander against Philotas in the course of his trial for conspiracy: that he did not deign to address the court 'in Macedonian' but insisted on showing off in Greek. And Alexander is at least once said to have addressed his troops 'in Macedonian'.

Those who favour the view that the Macedonians were Greeks regard this as evidence, not for a separate Macedonian language, but for the use of dialect in certain circumstances, comparable to the use of Scots in a British regiment consisting largely of Scots.

In favour of the Greek identity of the Macedonians is what we know of their language: the place-names, names of the

11

months and personal names, which are without exception Greek in roots and form. This suggests that they did not merely use Greek as a lingua franca, but spoke it as natives (though with a local accent which turned Philip into Bilip, for example). The Macedonians' own traditions derived their royal house from one Argeas, son of Macedon, son of Zeus, and asserted that a new dynasty, the Temenids, had its origin in the sixth century from emigrants from Argos in Greece, the first of these kings being Perdiccas. This tradition became a most important part of the cultural identity of Macedon. It enabled Alexander I (d.452) to compete at the Olympic Games (which only true Hellenes were allowed to do); and it was embedded in the policy of Archelaus (d.399) who invited Euripides from Athens to his court, where Euripides wrote not only the *Bacchae* but also a lost play called *Archelaus*. (Socrates was also invited, but declined.) It was in keeping with this background that Philip employed Aristotle – who had until then been helping Hermias of Atarneus in the Troad to rule as a Platonic 'philosopher-king' – as tutor to his son, and that Alexander grew up with a devotion to Homer and the Homeric world which his own kingship so much recalled, and slept every night with the *Iliad* under his pillow.

The Macedonians, then, were racially Greek. The relation might be not so much that of British and Scots as of Germans and Austrians; but in the case of Macedon it was the smaller partner which effected the *Anschluss*, as Philip's reign was devoted to gaining control not only of the northern Aegean but of the city-states of mainland Greece, too.

The Macedon into which Alexander was born was becoming an international power under his father's rule. Philip had acceded to the throne in 359 at the age of 24. His first action was to reorganise the army – the army which Alexander inherited and with which he conquered half of Asia. The key element of this army was the infantry phalanx, each member of which was armed with an enormously long spear or pike known as a *sarissa*. Approximately 5½ metres in length, the sarissas were carried horizontally by the soldiers as they advanced in rows, maybe ten deep, so that a slanting wall of spikes confronted the enemy before they were near enough to wield their swords. Other units were also involved, notably cavalry but also the élite *hypaspists*, or shield-bearers; and Philip also seized the

12

opportunity offered by contemporary developments in siege machinery, which was to be crucial to many of Alexander's successes.

With this formidable and well-trained army Philip quickly subdued the northern regions, including the former Athenian possession of Amphipolis. He then turned his attention to Greece proper, securing first the northern regions of Thessaly and Phocis. His designs on Greece have been made memorable by Demosthenes' numerous speeches warning his fellow-Athenians of Philip's ultimate intentions; but others in Athens favoured a policy of appeasement, and the elderly pamphleteer Isocrates saw in Philip a great hope – namely that he would lead a Greek crusade to take vengeance on the Persians for their destructive invasion of Greece in the early fifth century. His *Address to Philip* of 346, propounding just this idea, probably coincided with Philip's ultimate ambition rather than suggesting to him an idea that had never so far occurred to him. In due course the Persian king Artaxerxes became aware of Philip's plans and began to prepare for war, buying up Greek mercenaries in large numbers. By the end of 345 a large army had captured Sidon and was on its way to subdue Egypt, which was under the rule of a nationalist regime at whose head was the pharaoh Nectanebo. Nectanebo fled, Egypt capitulated, and Philip made a non-aggression pact with Persia (343) – for the time being.

Alexander was by this time 13 years old. He had been born in 356 to Philip's third wife, Olympias. Philip had several wives, all acquired for dynastic reasons: Olympias was the daughter of Neoptolemus of Epirus. She was the first to produce a son, and jealously guarded Alexander's succession when Philip in due course took two more wives. The last, Cleopatra, a relative of Attalus, may have been a love-match; certainly Olympias lost no time, when necessity arose, of eliminating her and her infant son Caranus, a potential rival to Alexander. Olympias was a strong-minded and formidable woman, and Alexander remained devoted to her and in awe of her all his life.

Philip and Olympias had first met at the Sanctuary of the Great Gods of Samothrace, while the Mysteries were being celebrated there. It seems that Olympias was a devotee of some remarkable cults which included the veneration of serpents and perhaps snake-handling. Thus legends arose about Alexander's

13

birth: that he was not really the son of Philip at all, but had been conceived by Olympias as the result of coupling with a snake. This became enhanced by the idea that the snake was an incarnation of the god Ammon. This idea of a divine birth was elaborated by the author of the *Alexander Romance* in the story that Alexander was actually the son of the pharaoh Nectanebo, who had fled Egypt for Macedon, persuaded Olympias to allow him into her bed by giving her prophecies about Ammon's choice of her as bride, and then entered her room at night with a pair of ram's horns strapped to his head and a purple cloak on his back to have intercourse with her.

The *Romance* makes this a reason for Philip's doubt of Alexander's legitimacy, but other sources also make clear his suspicion of the lad, or perhaps of the ambition of Olympias. However, he had him brought up and educated as a future king deserved, bringing Aristotle, the leading intellectual of his day, from Atarneus to Pella to be his tutor, and then transferring the educational establishment to the more remote region of the Gardens of Midas near Beroea (Verria). The other pupils included several high-born Macedonian youths: Hephaestion, son of Amyntor, who was to remain Alexander's closest friend; Cassander, son of Antipater, and Ptolemy, son of Lagus – both future kings; and Marsyas of Pella, who later wrote a book about Alexander. Plutarch (who had access to Alexander's correspondence) tells us that, besides the study of the poems of Homer – the fundamental of any Greek education – Aristotle instructed Alexander in ethics and politics 'but also in those secret and more esoteric studies which philosophers do not impart to the general run of students, but only by word of mouth to a select circle of the initiated' (Plut. *Alex*. 7.5). This may be imagination; but Plutarch also tells us that 'It was Aristotle, I believe, who did more than anyone to implant in Alexander his interest in the art of healing as well as that of philosophy' (Plut. *Alex*. 8). Plutarch is concerned to paint a somewhat glowing picture of the young man with philosophic interests like Plutarch's own; but it seems plain that the retinue of scientists Alexander took with him to Asia owed something to the love of learning instilled in him by Aristotle. Aristotle wrote two now lost works, 'On kingship' and 'To Alexander, concerning [or, on behalf of] the colonies', which surely focused on the requirements of the future king; the latter in particular is likely to have reflected Aristotle's view that the barbarian nations, like cattle, need the hand of a cultured person (i.e. a Greek) to get the best out of them – an idea which chimed well with ideas of Asiatic conquest current at the Macedonian court. Ehrenberg (1938) believed that these ideas influenced Alexander's actual practice in ruling the peoples he conquered, but the evidence suggests rather, as we shall see, that, for all his love of Greek culture, Greek rule of other peoples was the last thing he sought, and even Macedonian hegemony was much tempered by his use of native governors.

A second teacher of Alexander was Leonidas, a kinsman of his mother, who subjected him to a tough physical regime, but who is mainly remembered for the jibe Alexander directed at him after his first conquests. Leonidas had bidden his pupil be sparing with the frankincense until he had conquered the land that produced it; when he did so, Alexander sent him an enormous quantity of it (Plutarch, *Sayings of Kings and Commanders*, 4).

It was during Alexander's schooldays that he acquired his famous horse Bucephalas, who was to accompany him all the way to India. The story is told by Plutarch and the *Alexander Romance* as an example of the young prince's precocious ability. A particularly uncontrollable horse was brought as a gift to Philip (wilder versions say that it ate human flesh). Everyone was afraid of it, but Alexander spotted that the creature was rearing at its shadow, turned it away from the sun, soothed it and at last mounted it. The anecdote casts a nice light on his undoubted abilities to manage both men and beasts, and to succeed where others had failed.

Alexander's physical appearance was striking, even if he was not as romantically handsome as the multitudinous sculpted portraits imply. Like Napoleon, he was rather short. According to the *Alexander Romance*, his eyes were of different colours. This piece of information, combined with the characteristic twist of the neck and heavenward glance in most of the statues, has been taken as an indication of 'ocular torticollis', a posture of the head which compensates for the palsy of one eye. Thus a handicap became in art an emblem of kingship.

In 338 began Philip's final act of conquest against Greece. Athens and Thebes, holding the line for the rest of Greece, were defeated at the battle of Chaeronea (August), an event which spelled the end of Greek freedom. Alexander, now 18, commanded the cavalry on the left wing who were to deliver the decisive blow in the battle. Following the battle, a Hellenic League (the name recalled that of the League of 480 which had resisted the Persians), also known as the League of Corinth, was formed under Philip's leadership – a polite way of indicating that Philip now controlled Greece. In autumn 337 the plan of a military expedition against Persia was ratified at a meeting at Corinth, and in the following spring Philip's generals Parmenio (400–327) and Attalus (390–334; the uncle of Philip's wife Cleopatra) were sent to Asia Minor to undertake preliminary operations. Parmenio was the greatest of Philip's generals – Philip said of him, 'The Athenians elect ten generals every year, but I have found only one general – Parmenio' (Heckel 1992, 13) – and continued in loyal service to Alexander, too, until his elimination in 330. Shortly after this expedition departed, Artaxerxes died and was succeeded as king of Persia by Darius III.

Everything appeared to be moving steadily forward according to Philip's plans. But there were tensions at home. In 338 Philip had married Cleopatra (Eurydice), as mentioned above – an act which clearly drove Olympias to wild jealousy and which prompted a mighty row between Alexander and his father at the wedding banquet, which as usual in Macedonian festivities involved massive consumption of strong wine. Cleopatra's uncle Attalus called on the assembled company to pray 'that the union of Philip and Cleopatra might bring forth a legitimate heir to the throne'. Alexander, insulted at the slur on his legitimacy, hurled a cup at him. Philip drew his sword against his son, but fell over a table before he could do any harm. Alexander promptly left for Illyria, and Olympias went away to Epirus. Whether they had any part in what followed can never be known, but plainly both were in a vulnerable position, which became the more exposed when Cleopatra gave birth to a son in summer 336. Bosworth (1971a) has suggested that there are dynastic implications in these events as well as the overt personal jealousies: Cleopatra, from an old Macedonian family, represented the élite of Lower Macedonia, while Olympias, an Epirot, was an outsider. This would explain the taunt about Alexander's legitimacy, and also Olympias' departure to Epirus, the location of her supporting groups. The period was obviously riven with tensions about who would succeed Philip, and the obscure episode in which Pixodarus, the dynast of Caria, made overtures to marry his daughter to Alexander's mentally defective half-brother Arrhidaeus must also have a place in the complex of events, though its precise significance is impossible to unravel.

However, Alexander was soon back in favour, or at least in position in Pella. Philip, on the point of departing for Asia, needed to secure Macedonia behind him. Alexander was recalled from Illyria to act as regent. In what seemed a gesture of peace, Philip offered the hand of his daughter by Olympias, Cleopatra (to be distinguished from his wife Cleopatra) to the king of Epirus, also called Alexander ('Alexander the Molossian'), who was also her uncle. The purpose may, however, have been to marginalise Olympias by constructing an independent link between Philip's family and that of the Epirot king. A great celebration was planned at the Macedonian capital of Aegae (modern Vergina). Visitors came from all over Greece. The second day of the celebrations was given over to games, which took place in Aegae's theatre. Philip entered the theatre in simple pomp, clad in a white cloak and flanked on the one side by his son Alexander, on the other by his new son-in-law Alexander. The bodyguard was instructed to follow at a little distance. As he paused for the crowd's acclaim a member of the bodyguard, one Pausanias, rushed forward and stabbed Philip. Pausanias was quickly seized and speared by a group of nobles; but Philip had died instantly.

Pausanias' motive was known. (Diodorus reports the details: and Satyrus, the contemporary author of a book on Philip, was the source.) He had been favoured by Philip as his lover, but Philip had transferred his attentions to another young man. Pausanias had then been thoroughly humiliated by a gang-rape arranged by Attalus, Philip's father-in-law. Philip had declined to do anything about it, and Pausanias had committed this murder through jealousy. The motive, though no doubt real, scarcely seems sufficient for so public an act with such inescapable consequences for the perpetrator. Suspicion has often arisen that this story was an 'official version' and that something more lay behind the assassination – either a Persian plot, or the hand of Olympias and Alexander himself. Another possibility is a dynastic plot by Alexander the Lyncestian to oust Cleopatra's offspring and ensure Alexander's succession before Caranus was grown up. Certainly the Lyncestians were prominent in the aftermath of the murder. Lurid stories circulated, that Olympias placed a gold crown on the corpse of Pausanias where it hung exposed, nailed to a gibbet, and that she poured libations on the spot each year on the anniversary of the murder. Nothing now can be certain, but it was Olympias' family who benefited, as Alexander at once became undisputed king. Persia, however, gained no benefit at all from replacing the hostility of Philip with that of Alexander. The crusade against Persia moved into a higher gear.

Philip was buried as befitted a king. If the tomb discovered at Vergina (Aegae) by Manolis Andronikos in his excavations in 1977–8 is really that of Philip, we know exactly where he lay, behind a plastered wall frescoed with a scene of Persephone's descent into the underworld. Some of the grave goods, including the unequal greaves (Philip was lame), as well as the skull with a massive cut across the left eye (in which Philip was blind), indicate that the occupant of the tomb was Philip. Many archaeologists, however, believe that the tomb is that of a later Macedonian king, perhaps Arrhidaeus. The miniature ivory heads of Philip and Alexander found in the tomb seem neatly to symbolise what with hindsight was seen as the inevitable succession.

3

The consolidation of Alexander's rule

Alexander's first task as king was to secure his position. Whatever his own role in the assassination of Philip, there were others who might be expected to take advantage of Philip's death to make a bid for the throne. So, despite the acclamation of the young man as king, he took steps to eliminate possible rivals. Plutarch (Plut. *de fort. Alex.* 1.3) says that at this time 'all Macedonia was looking to the sons of Aeropus'. One of these, Alexander of Lyncestis, was son-in-law of Antipater and hastened to swear loyalty to Alexander, and thus survived. But his two brothers were immediately put to death. Two of the sons of the youngest Lyncestian, Arrhabaios, held significant commands in Alexander's army in Asia, though according to Arrian (Arr. *Anab.* 1.20.1) the younger of them, Neoptolemus, defected to Darius; Diodorus (Diod. Sic. 17.25.5) has a different story. Alexander the Lyncestian himself was accused of treasonable correspondence with Darius in winter 334 and placed under close arrest; he was eventually executed in 330 in the aftermath of the conspiracy of Philotas. There was evidently no love lost between these two families.

The younger Lyncestians may have been executed less because they represented a direct threat than because they might support the stronger rival claims of Amyntas, the son of Perdiccas. Amyntas himself was a likely pretender to the throne, and was disposed of within the year, and probably much sooner.

19

Two of Philip's most loyal generals, Parmenio and Attalus, were away conducting operations in Asia Minor. Though Alexander repeatedly distanced himself from Parmenio, the general seems to have made a point of loyalty to his king throughout his career. Attalus (who was married to Parmenio's daughter) was a different matter. He was engaged in treasonable correspondence with Athens soon after Philip's death; Parmenio refused to play along, but before Attalus could switch his allegiance to Alexander he was assassinated by an emissary from Alexander, Hecataeus. The infant Caranus waited a little longer to be dispatched; in the first half of 335, while Alexander was campaigning in Illyria, he sent orders to his mother to dispose of the boy. Olympias outdid her instructions by savagely murdering both Caranus and his little sister; their mother Cleopatra either was murdered, too, or hanged herself. Alexander now remained the sole representative of the royal house, apart from his half-brother Philip Arrhidaeus (son of Philip's mistress Philinna), who was mentally defective in some way.

The second urgent task facing Alexander involved the Greek states. These reacted to the news of Philip's death with unrest bordering on insurrection. In Athens, Demosthenes voted a gold crown to Philip's assassin and entered (as we have seen) into correspondence with Attalus to overthrow Alexander. Alexander's advisers, chief among whom was Antipater (the father of his fellow-pupil in Aristotle's school, Cassander), urged caution. But Alexander immediately marched south for Greece. Finding the Vale of Tempe blocked by Thessalian defenders, Alexander did not wait to parley, but had steps cut in Mount Ossa and marched his entire army around the seaward crags. At this the Thessalians conceded defeat and acknowledged Macedonian rule by electing Alexander as their *tagos* ('leader'). It is the first example of Alexander's astonishing capacity for inventing unusual military stratagems to achieve his ends.

The Amphictyonic Council in Phocis quickly acknowledged his mastery of Greece. Thebes, Athens and Megara quietly played along too. Only Sparta politely insisted that 'their ancient traditions did not allow them to serve a foreign leader'; but they did not look like making trouble. Alexander's progress into Greece ended at Corinth where he was acknowledged as leader of the Hellenic League, and thus of the war against Persia.

But before he returned to Macedonia two interesting and significant events took place.

The first was his encounter with the Cynic philosopher Diogenes. The Cynics (the name means 'dog-like') set themselves against normal human standards and aimed to live 'in accordance with nature' by eschewing such comforts as beds and drinking-vessels. Diogenes himself lived, more or less naked, in a barrel in Corinth and was said to be in the habit of prowling the streets with a lamp in broad daylight, 'looking for a good man'. He is supposed to have died of choking while attempting to prove some point by eating a raw octopus. Cynics followed the example of Socrates in presenting themselves as irritants to the body politic, and had a fondness for annoying verbal and mathematical quibbling. Some scholars have imagined that they were influenced by the habits of Indian ascetics, of the kind Alexander encountered later at Taxila. This is perhaps unlikely, but there are points of similarity, as there are also with the hippies of the 1960s. Anything less like Alexander's passion for worldly power, and his curiosity, would be hard to imagine. An encounter so piquant 'had to happen'. The source is probably Onesicritus who took an interest in Cynic philosophy (see Chapter 7). Even if the episode is pure fiction, as most scholars have concluded, it became one of the most enduring traditions about Alexander and a symbol of the contrast between two ways of life.

It was curiosity that led Alexander to Diogenes. He looked at him. Diogenes said nothing. Eventually Alexander asked Diogenes if he would request a favour from the great king. 'Yes,' said Diogenes, 'please stand aside. You are blocking my sunshine.' Alexander was apparently impressed. 'If I were not Alexander,' he said, 'I would like to be Diogenes.'

A second event which might cast light on Alexander's character followed shortly afterwards, when he visited the oracle at Delphi. He arrived in the winter season (it was late November) when the god Apollo was held to be away feasting with the Hyperboreans and the oracle did not operate. But Alexander would not be gainsaid. He dragged the prophetess into the shrine and demanded an oracle. 'Young man,' she gasped as she struggled from the floor, 'no one can resist you!' Alexander accepted this as a thoroughly satisfactory oracle, gave a gift to the temple, and returned to Macedonia. The anecdote demonstrates the importance attached by Alexander to divine support and approval throughout his career. Again, however, it is almost certainly fictional: the source is probably Cleitarchus.

Back in Macedonia a new military task awaited him: the suppression of revolts, first by the Thracians and Triballians, based south of the Danube in Bulgaria, then by the Getae north of the Danube, and finally by the Illyrians, who occupied an area roughly corresponding to modern Albania. Tactics and efficiency, rather than military strength, enabled Alexander to beat all these opponents, and the Triballian king offered his allegiance to Macedon, to be quickly followed by the other peoples.

Alexander's absence in the north-west gave the Greek states the opportunity to develop new resistance. Demosthenes spread a rumour – even producing a bloodstained messenger – that Alexander had been slaughtered by the Triballians; and, more alarmingly, the Persian king had sent gold to Athens to support the resistance to Alexander. He also stepped up his action against the activities of Parmenio in Asia Minor, employing his most skilled commander, a Greek mercenary named Memnon of Rhodes, to drive Parmenio back from the land he had won in the Troad. Thebes, encouraged by Demosthenes' disinformation, was in open revolt.

Within two weeks Alexander's army was at the gates of Thebes. The city, this time, was not in placable mood. Its leaders were determined to fight to the last for freedom. Their heralds openly called for any who wished 'to join the Great King and Thebes in freeing the Greeks' to come over to them. Alexander's response was complete destruction of the city. After a fierce battle fought before the walls, entry was gained through a postern. Alexander's army rushed through the city, killing and looting, raping and burning. When the fighting was over, with 6000 Thebans dead, and 30,000 taken prisoner, Alexander called a meeting of the Hellenic League to decide on its fate. One imagines that they did not argue with his proposals. The city was razed to the ground – except for the temples and the house of the lyric poet Pindar, already one of the classic authors of Greek literature, who had died some 120 years before – and the remaining inhabitants were sold into slavery, except for priests and known supporters of Macedon.

Athens was now in a panic. Debate in the assembly revolved around the decision whether to resist or to surrender. Alexander had demanded the surrender of ten generals, but the orator Demades led an embassy to Pella in which he succeeded in having this order rescinded. (Alexander, however, insisted on the exile of one of the ten, Charidemus, who promptly took refuge in Persia.) Athens played along with Alexander, as did the other Greek states, but they never welcomed his rule.

With Greek resistance annihilated, Alexander was ready to turn his full attention to the crusade against Persia which had been his father's ambition and was to become the dominant motif of his own career. Why did he undertake this?

4

The war in Asia Minor

The Persian Empire – or the Empire of the Medes, as the Greeks called it – had been founded by Cyrus the Great, king of Persis (in southern Iran), in 559 when he conquered Media (the north-west mountain region of Iran around Hamadan). In the 540s Cyrus gained control of Asia Minor including the kingdom of Lydia and the Greek cities of the Aegean coast (Ionia). In 529, Cyrus was succeeded by his son Cambyses, who brought Egypt under Persian rule. The long reign of Cambyses' successor Darius (521–486) was interrupted by an unsuccessful revolt of the Ionian Greeks in 499. The involvement of Athens and Eretria in this revolt prompted a campaign against Greece in which the Persians were decisively defeated by the combined forces of the Greeks at the battle of Marathon (September 490). But when Darius' son Xerxes came to the throne he prepared new plans for the conquest of Greece. Again the Greeks defeated the Persians in a series of great battles, by sea at Salamis (480) and later at Mycale (479), and by land at Plataea (479), where Thebes had fought on the Persian side. However, the Persian sack of Athens, and burning of the temples on the Acropolis, in 480 was a never-forgotten slight, and resistance to the Persians became one of the defining features of Greek identity. Even after 150 years, the 'enslavement' of the Ionian Greeks to Persia still rankled with mainland Greeks. So Greek opinion would always be favourable to a crusade against the ancestral enemy. It would

24

be a main plank of Macedon's claim to leadership of the Greeks, and to Greek identity, that the kingdom shared this ambition.

Darius' empire was a vast agglomeration of territory which included not only all of present-day Iran, but also the whole of Asia Minor, all of the Levant from the Zagros to the sea, and Egypt. Eastwards it incorporated Afghanistan and may have extended fingers of control into the Indus valley; it also included parts of Central Asia at least as far as the River Oxus. Naturally this enormous territory was not subject to a strong centralised control. Administration was in the hands of regional rulers, known as satraps, and in the further eastern regions local princes and dynasts ruled under fealty to Persia. Despite its vast size, the empire was held together by a highly efficient system of communications, the lynchpin of which was the Royal Road from Sardis to Susa, which was provided with post stations for mounted couriers at regular intervals. The ceremonial capital of the empire was Persepolis, while Cyrus the Great was buried at nearby Parsagarda; but the court spent much of its time at Babylon at the junction of the Tigris and Euphrates (near Baghdad), retiring from its overpowering summer heat to the mountain city of Ecbatana (Hamadan) in Media.

Alexander had probably inherited from his father the limited aim of freeing the Greeks of Asia Minor – and that is precisely what Parmenio and Attalus had been doing in the Troad (whether the Greeks liked being liberated or not). But both Alexander and Philip must have realised that geography prevented permanent Greek military control of the Aegean seaboard. Once a land-based power determined to secure that region (just as Atatürk's Turkey did in the 1920s), it was impossible for the maritime power of Greece to withstand it. So the aim quickly became the defeat of the Persian king on terms that would admit of a permanent political cession of his western lands. As Alexander's successes multiplied, ambition became steadily greater; but his minimum aim when he set out must have been to compel Darius to acknowledge without question Greek authority over the regions he chose to conquer.

The campaign began in spring 334. Alexander's army consisted of at least 30,000 infantry and 5000 cavalry; but he was able to leave an infantry force of comparable size, and about 1500 cavalry, in Greece and Macedon to maintain security. He also had a fleet of 120 warships as well as a number of

25

cargo-ships. Antipater was left as regent in Macedon and as deputy leader of the Hellenic League.

The army reached the Hellespont (Dardanelles) in twenty days, and the crossing into Asia began. This was a time-consuming operation, and while Parmenio took charge of it Alexander undertook a detour which was of great propaganda value as well as religious significance. It began with a sacrifice at the tomb of Protesilaus (the name means 'first-leaper'), who had been the first of the Greeks to land when the Trojan War began – and the first to die too. Alexander then crossed the straits of Gallipoli. Hurling his spear into the soil of Asia as he landed, he claimed the entire territory as 'spear-won land', set up altars to the gods, and set off for Troy. Here he was welcomed by the local Greeks. He made sacrifice at what then (and now) purported to be the tombs of the Greek heroes Achilles and Ajax, and then engaged in a race with his friend Hephaestion around the tombs of Achilles and Patroclus, friends as inseparable in their day as Alexander and Hephaestion were to be now. Here, too, according to the *Romance* (1.42), a local poet offered to write a poem about Alexander which would outdo Homer's celebration of Achilles. Alexander's caustic reply was: 'I would rather be a Thersites in Homer than an Agamemnon in *your* poetry.' This series of events indicates not only Alexander's admiration for – even obsession with – the poems of Homer, but also his deliberate claim to be avenging a slight that went back not merely to the Persian conquest, but to the Trojan War, the first clash of Greeks and Asiatics. He dedicated his own armour in the temple of Athena, and took instead a set purportedly from the days of the Trojan War, which he carried as a talisman ever afterwards.

The crossing of the Hellespont completed, the army moved forward cautiously; while the Persian high command, some 100 kilometres to the west at Zeleia, debated its next move. The Persian army, despite its immense cavalry, some 20,000 strong, was comparatively weak in foot soldiers; the best of the latter were probably the Greek mercenaries (again about 20,000 in number). Memnon, the Greek mercenary general of the Persian forces, favoured a scorched earth policy, destroying all possibility of provisioning in front of Alexander's army; but the local satrap objected. In the end the army advanced and took up a position on the eastern bank of the River Granicus. Here

Alexander fought his first pitched battle against the Persian enemy.

The sources differ as to precisely what took place. Those which most favour Alexander suggest that he undertook an action which might appear impossible. The Persian troops were assembled at the top of a steep, muddy, slippery bank. Arrian and Plutarch describe a direct assault, in the late afternoon, across the river, up the banks, and through the Persian lines to victory. Diodorus, however, reports a dawn manoeuvre in which the army moved downstream to a shallower crossing-place and outflanked the Persian army, catching them by surprise. Interestingly, this is precisely the manoeuvre represented by Arrian as advised by Parmenio. If Alexander was following the road to the satrapal capital, he is likely to have been led by that road to an easier ford (Foss 1977). One may suspect that an encomiastic tradition has attributed to Alexander a more heroic action and one which (like many other anecdotes) shows Parmenio as a ditherer in contrast to Alexander's brilliant impetuosity. Diodorus, who is often regarded as unreliable by those who regard the Arrian tradition as paramount, has preserved an account which at least is susceptible of possibility.

The decisive engagement was a heroic clash of cavalry in which Alexander fought in the thick. He came close to death and was saved by Cleitus, the commander of the Royal Squadron, who severed his assailant's arm as it descended to strike Alexander a mortal blow. After routing the Persian horse, the Macedonian cavalry easily surrounded the Persian and mercenary infantry. The slaughter was heavy, and eight of the Persian commanders were killed. Arsites, the senior surviving Persian general, committed suicide. Alexander had won his battle, and Asia Minor lay open before him.

Quickly he swept down the Ionian coast, with an initial detour inland to Sardis, capital of the Persian satrapy of Lydia. The governor, Mithrines, surrendered before Alexander had even reached the walls, and Alexander was able to take possession of the treasure stored in its acropolis. Philip had made Macedon immeasurably wealthier than it had been before; but an expedition like Alexander's needed exceptional resources, and the capture of bullion was an important strategic element at this stage of the march, as was the securing of this key to the satrapy's supply system. The satrap, Spithridates, was replaced by Parmenio's brother Asander; in addition Alexander appointed a new city governor, Pausanias, and a finance officer, Nicias.

The cities of Ephesus, Magnesia and Tralles welcomed Alexander without a struggle, and the watchword of 'liberation of the Greeks' was put into effect with the 'restoration' of 'democracies' in what had been oligarchically controlled cities. The policy was the opposite of that employed in Greece, where oligarchic groups favourable to Macedon were imposed on the cities; but in both cases it depended on installing a new governing class whose loyalty was to Macedon as their guarantor. The Persian tribute was abolished; the cities promised henceforth to pay 'contributions' to their new leader. Some subtler minds may have been able to make the distinction between this and tribute. Garrisons were also installed in all the cities in this war zone.

It is a much disputed question whether these cities became members of the Hellenic League (League of Corinth). In fact there is no evidence either way. A more important question is what this 'liberation' of the cities consisted in. For Droysen, as Badian neatly put it, Alexander was a proto-Bismarck, creating 'free Imperial cities' like Hamburg within the empire. Wilcken and Berve assumed that the cities simply became part of the League – the 'contribution' (*syntaxis*) being a commutation of their duty of military obligations. Tarn took the starry-eyed view that the cities were left completely free and autonomous, an interpretation which flies in the face of known facts, not least what happened to Aspendus when it havered over the price demanded for its 'freedom': Alexander had preparations under way for a siege before the leaders changed their mind (and then doubled their contribution). As Badian sums it up, the cities were to be free on condition that they obeyed Alexander. Greek cities and non-Greek cities, like Sardis, were treated alike, and administrative arrangements were left largely unchanged; their laws were 'restored' as Arrian (Arr. *Anab.* 1.18.2) puts it: Alexander had more important issues on his mind, and obedience was all that was required. Bosworth takes a more lenient view than Badian of Alexander's behaviour here (1988, 252–4): the settlement of Priene, for example, is 'generous' – but only because it did not matter militarily.

Alexander wanted to leave a permanent mark of his visit at Ephesus, and offered to restore the temple of Artemis which, according to tradition, had been burned down on the night of Alexander's birth by a madman named Herostratus who wished thus to make his name immortal. (He succeeded.) But the Ephesians diplomatically replied that 'It was not right for one god to dedicate a temple to another' (Strabo 14.1.22), and the offer was refused. Alexander had better luck at Priene, which had to be forcibly liberated: here he made a contribution to the cost of building the new temple of Athena Polias, and his assistance was recorded on a large inscription (now in the British Museum).

Miletus also resisted liberation, preferring a neutral status, but was quickly persuaded by Alexander's siege engines. All this time there was no activity by the Persian army, but Memnon's forces were tracking Alexander by sea. Alexander's small fleet declined any engagement with them, and so Memnon's presence proved quite ineffective. This seems to have been the reason why Alexander now decided that he could do without his fleet, and disbanded it. It was expensive and, manned as it was by Greeks, of dubious loyalty. This decision laid on him the necessity of capturing all the harbours of the eastern Mediterranean in order to secure his rear, and this is what he proceeded to do. But the decision to do without a fleet proved a short-sighted one.

Alexander now advanced into Caria. The Persians under Memnon had regrouped in its chief city, Halicarnassus, which was under the rule of a Carian dynasty. The legitimate queen, Ada, had been ousted by her brother Pixodarus; he had recently died, and rule was now in the hands of his son-in-law, a Persian named Orontobates. Alexander's strategy of 'liberation' took him to Ada's inland stronghold of Alinda, where he pledged his support to her cause, and she made him her adoptive son. The other Carian cities welcomed him with open arms as he crossed the Euromus range and descended to the coast, approaching the high walls and citadel of Halicarnassus from the north-west. There was a short delay while he waited for the transport-ships with his siege engines to arrive; once they did, they made short work of the walls. Many of the defenders were killed. In the course of the night, Memnon and Orontobates set fire to the remaining buildings and evacuated the city, though they retained control of the citadel. Alexander razed to the ground what was left of the city and restored Ada as queen with a substantial garrison force. He felt secure enough to advance, but Memnon was still at large.

The next stage of the march was to establish control of the southern coast of Asia Minor and remove all power from the enemy fleet. Parmenio, however, was sent back to Sardis to undertake campaigns against the peoples of central Anatolia. By midwinter 334/3, Alexander was at Phaselis, and here a curious piece of intelligence arrived from Parmenio. The latter had captured a Persian named Sisines, who had brought to Alexander the Lyncestian (currently serving in Parmenio's forces) a letter from Darius offering 1000 talents for the murder of King Alexander. When Sisines told his story to the king, Alexander was uncertain what to believe. Could it be just a plot by Parmenio to discredit a possible rival? Or was it true? Alexander was later to claim that Olympias had been warning him in letters about the Lyncestian for some time. Alexander took the precaution of having his namesake arrested and kept under close guard, but he was allowed to live until he was implicated in the alleged conspiracy of Philotas in late 330.

This problem disposed of, Alexander moved along the coast into Pamphylia: the troops marched over Mount Climax along a road specially constructed by pioneers, but Alexander and his staff travelled along the coast. At one point the sea washed against the cliffs and over the narrow path; but the wind veered to the north and cleared the route for the king. The historian Callisthenes was able to make the most of this event, as being an acknowledgement by the elements themselves of their new master, making obeisance before him.

The remaining cities of the region – Termessus, Aspendus, Perge, Selge and Sagalassus – were quickly secured, and Alexander now prepared to cross the mountains to rejoin Parmenio at Gordium. He had to pass Celaenae, a stage on the Royal Road, and leave it secure behind him. But the city was impregnable and ready for a siege. Alexander was in a hurry. He therefore left one of his generals, Antigonus the One-Eyed, to guard the region, and covered the 130 miles to Gordium, arriving in March 333. The city surrendered immediately. With the arrival of Parmenio's forces, probably in April, the Macedonian army was reunited.

But the news from the west was not good. Memnon had reoccupied many of the Aegean islands and may have been planning to invade Greece directly via Euboea. Alexander was constrained to commission a new fleet – an expense he had hoped to avoid – and to send commanders back to the Greek field of war.

In Gordium he had the opportunity of a major propaganda coup. In the palace of the legendary King Gordius, founder of the Phrygian kingdom, was a wagon whose yoke was fastened to its pole by a knot of cornel bark, the ends of which were invisible. An ancient tradition, perhaps invented for the occasion, said that whoever could undo this knot would become lord of all Asia. Alexander contemplated the problem for a while and then, with his usual impetuous disregard for little difficulties, cut through the knot with his sword. Callisthenes was quick to hail this achievement as proof of divine endorsement for the campaign.

A further proof of divine favour was surely the opportune death of Memnon from sickness, which took place at about this time. Its result was that Darius gave no further thought to a possible European campaign. The Persians remained in control of the Aegean, but the Persian strategy now centred on a new direct land clash with Alexander – and that was a strategy which suited Alexander, too.

While Darius was awaiting the arrival of fresh troops at Babylon, Alexander hastened through the Anatolian uplands into Cilicia; forcing his way through the lightly defended Cilician Gates, he arrived at Tarsus on 3 September 333 after covering the last 55 kilometres in a single day. Hot and exhausted, he plunged into the River Cydnus for a refreshing swim, and was immediately taken ill. Cramps and a chill were followed by a high fever, and the king was laid up for several weeks. His private physician Philip prepared some medicine, presumably to bring the fever down; but a note arrived from Parmenio to the effect that Philip was planning to poison Alexander. Alexander read the letter, handed it to Philip to read, and drank the medicine. Fortunately it had the desired result, though its effects were violent to begin with, and Alexander pulled through. One wonders what Parmenio's intentions were in this odd episode.

By now Darius had assembled a huge army – an astonishing and improbable 600,000 according to Arrian (Arr. *Anab.* 2.8.6), including 30,000 Greek mercenaries (Bosworth 1988, 57) – and was marching steadily northwards from Babylon, accompanied by the royal treasure and the women of the court, including Darius' mother, wife and daughter. The impedimenta (though not the royal women) were left in safety at Damascus, and the army encamped at Sochi, a short distance inland from the coast of the Gulf of Iskenderun, but separated from it by the Amanus range.

Developments were slow as Alexander was still recovering from his illness. Presently he moved eastwards to Issus. Issus lies near the head of the Gulf of Iskenderun, commanding the entrance to a narrow coastal plain between the sea and the Amanus mountains which leads into Syria. Uncertain of Darius' position – as Darius was of Alexander's – the Macedonian king moved forward fast to a place called Myriandrus, near the head of the 'Syrian Gates'. He left his sick and wounded behind at Issus. What seems clear is that Alexander (if not Parmenio) anticipated attack only from the south, through the Syrian Gates. In fact Darius swept north around the Amanus range and descended on the camp at Issus. There, he captured the hospitalised soldiers and, after cutting off their hands and cauterising the stumps with pitch, sent them off to report to Alexander on the strength of the Persian forces. The Persian army now descended on Alexander from the north, in his rear.

The army which had just reached Myriandrus had to return to face an enemy which had taken it by surprise. Darius' army took up position behind the River Pinarus, somewhere to the south of Issus. There are several streams crossing this plain; the one concerned may have been the Kuru Cay, some 15 kilometres north of the narrowest part of the plain. So, as at the Granicus, a river lay between the armies. This proved disastrous for the Macedonian phalanx, which lost cohesion in the crossing and found itself engaged in hand-to-hand combat with the Persians' Greek mercenaries, in which the long sarissas were worse than useless. On the other hand, the narrowness of the plain meant that the Persian superior numbers, and cavalry, were of no advantage to them. At one point Alexander himself located Darius and was pursuing him with the determination of killing him – the moment portrayed in the famous mosaic from the House of the Faun at Pompeii. But Darius, seizing the reins of his chariot with his own hands, turned tail and had a considerable start. The Persian cavalry wavered and fled with

Darius, plunging through the infantry behind him. At the same time, the Macedonian phalanx regrouped and drove the mercenaries back from the stream. Soon the whole Persian army was in rout. However, evening was falling, and it proved impossible for Alexander's men to capture Darius.

The Macedonians quickly took control of the Persian camp with its valuable furniture, gold dinner service and 3000 talents of gold, as well as the royal ladies. Alexander took a bath in Darius' tub – which a courtier pointed out to him was now 'Alexander's tub' – and, as he settled on to a luxurious couch for dinner, remarked with irony: 'So this is what it is to be a king.' The same remark had been made by the Spartan regent Pausanias when he entered the tent of Mardonius 150 years before, according to Herodotus (9.82 cf. Athenaeus 4.15). Was it Alexander, or is it our source, Plutarch (*Alex*. 20), or his source, Cleitarchus, who is quoting the earlier author?

Darius' women were treated with the utmost chivalry, and continued to receive the allowances and attention they had when Darius was their master. They were valuable hostages, to be sure; but it seems, too, that Alexander had no interest in inflicting pain and humiliation for the sake of it. As would emerge later, Darius was for him a political and military opponent, but not for that reason a personal enemy to be degraded.

As a result of the battle of Issus, Alexander could feel great confidence in his ability to beat the Persian army in battle. But he had not yet won the war. Ten thousand mercenaries had got away to fight again; the king himself still lived and was at large; and the eastern satrapies still remained to give him their backing, the more readily as the conqueror came closer. It was uncertain exactly where Darius had gone. For the moment, Alexander's only choice was to continue advancing until another pitched battle could decide the issue. It was to be almost two years before that third, and decisive, battle took place.

5

Son of Ammon

Once he had crossed into Cilicia in summer 333, Alexander could no longer pose as the liberator of the Greeks. He had come beyond Greek territory; from here he must come as, in Persian eyes, a usurper. At this point it must have begun to cross his mind that he was on course to become ruler of the Persian Empire, even if it was still, first and foremost, military necessity that dictated his continuing advance. He could argue that Darius needed to be forced into acknowledging his authority over the conquered regions. Furthermore, he had not yet secured the coastline, and the logical next move was to march through the Levant. Egypt must necessarily be taken into allegiance, too. But not all that occurred in Egypt can be taken as having direct military significance. The visit to the oracle of Ammon in winter 332/1 may have been propaganda, it may have been piety, or it may have been adventure; whichever it was, it takes us into the realm of Alexander's psychology and of his impact on his contemporaries.

The road south from Issus posed few problems. Cilicia and Syria were left in the hands of two of the Companions, the picked close friends of the king who, in Homeric style, acted as his advisers, war council and, when necessary, military commanders. (Their numbers at this time were limited, but at the time of the marriages at Susa in February 324 there were ninety-two of them. These élite Companions must be distinguished from the Companion Cavalry, a division of the army and naturally a much larger body.) Parmenio was sent to secure the submission of Damascus and the Persian baggage-train. The island state of Aradus (Arwad) surrendered. At Marathus ('Amrit) envoys arrived from Darius pleading for terms and for the return of Darius' womenfolk (Arr. *Anab.* 2.14). But terms were no longer enough for Alexander, who replied haughtily that he had come to take revenge for the Persians' ancient aggression against Greece, and concluded with a demand to be addressed in future as 'Lord of Asia', and for Darius to come to him personally if he wished to negotiate.

> Ask for your mother, wife and children, and what you will, when you have come, and you will receive them. You shall have whatever you persuade me to give. And in future when you send to me, make your addresses to the king of Asia, and do not correspond as an equal, but tell me, as lord of all your possessions, what you need; otherwise I shall make plans to deal with you as a wrongdoer. But if you claim the kingship, stand your ground and fight for it, and do not flee, for I shall pursue you wherever you are.
>
> (Arr. *Anab.* 2.14.8–9)

Byblos and Sidon surrendered. It was to be expected that the island city of Tyre, the ancient Phoenician port, would do likewise. Alexander began by requesting permission to come and sacrifice to Melqart – whom the Greeks identified with Heracles – at his festival, which was now taking place, in February 332. The Tyrians, however, refused to allow Alexander within their city and suggested that he sacrifice in Old Tyre on the mainland. Tyre would thus preserve its neutrality, whereas to allow the king to lead the religious ceremony within their walls would be to acknowledge his sovereignty. They were prepared to offer alliance. But Alexander insisted on submission. The heralds he sent to negotiate a peaceful settlement were murdered by the Tyrians and thrown over the battlements. From this point, nothing but absolute conquest would satisfy Alexander.

The capture of Tyre was strategically unnecessary (though the Tyrian fleet was significant): a garrison on the mainland would have achieved his ends. The six-month siege shows him, once again, as a master of tactics and of the art of siege warfare, but one suspects impetuosity in the decision to undertake a full siege in the first place.

Again Alexander will have regretted his lack of a fleet. Tyre stood on an island half a mile offshore, and the channel between was as much as twenty feet deep in places. How could he bring rams or troops anywhere near its towering walls without ships? His answer was to build a causeway or mole from the mainland to the foot of the walls. Old Tyre provided the stones; timber was brought from the slopes of the Lebanon, and the mole began to creep forward. The Tyrians soon began to harry the builders with arrows and slingshot: Alexander had protective screens built against them. The Tyrians sent a fireship which burned them down along with much of Alexander's artillery: he had new towers and artillery built. But he needed ships. Fortunately the news of Issus had resulted in large-scale defections of Phoenician and other squadrons from the Persian fleet, and Alexander soon had an armada of over 100 ships which quickly blockaded Tyre on the seaward side. These attacked the walls with rams, while the artillery on the mole was now within range to bombard the eastern side. As the siege became more vicious, the Tyrians invented new weapons, such as cauldrons of sand and gravel which were heated until red hot and then tipped over the forces attempting to scale the walls. The final assault took place on 30 July, and Alexander's troops surged into the city. Their vengeance for their half-year's sufferings was as savage as the sack of Thebes. The king was spared, but 30,000 prisoners were sold into slavery, and 2000 of the defenders were crucified. (So at least says Curtius; the more austere, or more favourable, Arrian, though agreeing on the number of the enslaved, does not mention the crucifixions.) Alexander was at last able to complete his sacrifice in the temple of Melqart.

One key to the success of this operation was Alexander's provisioning of his troops. Foraging parties were regularly sent out into the neighbouring countryside; and at one point, the Jewish historian Josephus tells us, a message was sent to the high priest in Jerusalem asking for assistance and supplies. This embassy, which is not mentioned by the other sources, became the keystone of an elaborate Jewish legend according to which Alexander actually visited Jerusalem. According to this story, he had been vouchsafed a vision of the prophet Jeremiah, who had briefed him about what he would find there. When he arrived, the high priest and all his retinue had assembled on Mount Scopus to greet him. Alexander amazed his companions by kneeling down and making obeisance before the high priest; when challenged by a bystander, he explained that he had paid homage not to the priest, but to the One God whom he represented. The Jews then brought forth the Book of Daniel and read him the prophecy in chapter 8 which was supposed to apply to Alexander. The story is marked as fiction by this touch since the Book of Daniel was not written until nearly 200 years after Alexander's death; but it encapsulates an important strand of contemporary and later perception of the king. Despite his depredations in the Levant, he has remained a hero in Jewish lore. Possibly such legends in some way reflect Alexander's own religious preoccupations, which came ever more into play in these years in the Levant – as we shall see.

According to Arrian (Arr. *Anab.* 2.25.1), a new embassy arrived from Darius in the course of the siege of Tyre, this time bearing letters offering a ransom of 10,000 talents for the womenfolk, and the cession of all the territory west of the Euphrates, and the hand of his daughter in marriage to cement an alliance between the two kings. Parmenio 'told Alexander that he would be glad to stop the war on these terms without further risks. . . . Alexander answered Parmenio that he too would have done this if he had been Parmenio, but as he was Alexander, he would make the reply he actually made': namely that all Darius offered was already his for the taking if he wanted (Arr. *Anab.* 2.25.2–3).

This episode poses a problem as it is reported in closely similar terms by the other historians (Plut. *Alex.* 29.7–9, Curt. 4.11, Diod. Sic 17.54.1–5) as occurring on Alexander's return from Egypt, in summer 331, shortly before the battle of Gaugamela – though in these authors the proposed ransom is given as 30,000 talents. Most modern authorities accept the later date; while Hammond (1993, 62), insistent on the superior value of Arrian, based, as he believes, on the 'Royal Journals', prefers to have the exchange of letters at this juncture. He remarks that it is more plausible to suppose that the letters were part of a quick to-and-fro (Marathus: late 333; Tyre: mid-332) than that they were sent more than a year apart. But one might also suppose that Darius' letters were inspired on the second occasion by the imminence of battle; he may have hoped, as Alexander turned away to Egypt, that his problem had gone away. The question cannot be answered with certainty, and shows clearly how problems of interpretation may be bound up with general principles: in this case Hammond's assessment of Arrian and his belief in the 'Royal Journal' determine his evaluation of the evidence for the particular episode, while Bosworth (1988. 76) and Hamilton (1969. 76–7) weigh the sources against each other as of equal value and give primacy to the majority.

The news of the fall of Tyre ensured the ready submission of the rest of the coastal cities of the Levant. Only Gaza resisted, to be brought low by another siege. During the fighting Alexander received a severe arrow-wound in the shoulder and lost a lot of blood; when he dragged himself back to the battlefield, his leg was cracked by a catapult stone. His revenge, when the city was reduced after two months, was to slaughter 10,000 defenders and sell the women and children into slavery. The king of Gaza, Batis, a huge corpulent eunuch, was privileged to receive a death modelled on Achilles' terrible revenge on the dead body of Hector: Batis, still alive, was attached to a chariot by a rope passed through his ankles and dragged around the city walls until he was dead. The authority for this episode is Curtius (4.6.15f); a slightly different version is given in a fragment of Hegesias (*FGrHist*142F5), and it is not in Plutarch or Arrian. Hammond (1983. 124–8) argues that the source is Cleitarchus because of the connection with Achilles that is emphasised, and Bosworth (1988. 68) follows this view. Both Plutarch and Arrian (unlike the censorious Curtius) were inclined to paint a more glowing picture of Alexander, and so there is a probability that this gruesome story is true.

From here Alexander made rapidly for Egypt. The Egyptians, who had only recently suffered the reimposition of Persian rule, welcomed him with open arms as a liberator, and in November 332 he was (probably) crowned as pharaoh at Memphis. Only the *Alexander Romance* actually mentions a coronation, and it may be that no formal ceremony took place; Alexander was simply acknowledged as the latest in the line of rulers and provided with a royal titulary and cartouche. The *Alexander Romance*, building on the legend that Alexander was actually the son of the last pharaoh, Nectanebo, reports that Alexander was shown a large basalt statue of Nectanebo on which was inscribed 'The king who has fled will return to Egypt, no longer an old man but a young one, and will subject our enemies the Persians to us'. Like the legend of the Gordian knot, any such inscription is likely to have been hastily contrived for the present moment; but as the *Romance* bears many signs of Egyptian origin it may well preserve a genuine tradition about this visit.

Alexander, now hailed as a god-king and successor of the pharaoh, must have begun, in the light of his tremendous successes, to wonder whether he really was, in the terms of the ancient world, a superhuman being. The divinisation of mortals was only just coming into fashion: the Spartan general Lysander (d.395) had been the first to receive cult as a god (on Samos), but the example Alexander set later in his career was to become the norm for rulers for centuries to come. Here we see his first 'intimations of immortality' (to borrow the nicely apposite phrase Peter Green employs for one of his chapter titles). One can attribute to these considerations his decision to make a pilgrimage to the oracle of Ammon at Siwa, 300 miles to the west of Memphis in the Libyan desert.

Ammon was a god in the form of a man with ram's horns and was identified by the Greeks with Zeus; he had received worship in some Greek cities as early as the fifth century BC but was predominantly an Egyptian deity. The legends of Alexander's birth put it about that Olympias had actually borne him as a son to Ammon and not to Philip. Alexander wished to discover the truth about his parentage (Arrian, Curtius, Justin); he wished to surpass the achievements of Perseus and Heracles (Strabo, Arrian); Arrian (Arr. *Anab.* 6.19.4) indicates that he wished to ask Ammon to which gods he should sacrifice as his expedition progressed; and it is reasonable to assume that he also wanted the confirmation of an oracle before embarking on what he intended to do next, namely to found a city in his own name to be the administrative centre of Egypt (Welles 1962). Arrian and Plutarch place the foundation of Alexandria before the expedition to Siwa; but Curtius, Diodorus and the *Alexander Romance* have it afterwards, though without any explicit causal connection.

This visit to Siwa introduces us for the first time to the idea of Alexander's 'longing' (the Greek word is *pothos*: Arr. *Anab.* 3.3.1) which becomes a leitmotif of Arrian's account of his career from this point onwards. (Arrian had referred to *pothos* once already, at 1.3.5, when Alexander was seized with a 'longing' to cross the Danube. Curtius also refers to it frequently by the Latin term *ingens cupido*.) The word seems to imply a kind of romantic yearning, a desire ever to 'go beyond'; it may also be etymologically connected with a word meaning 'to pray', in which case there would be a religious dimension to his yearning also. The term recurs in connection with the exploration of the east; here, as then, it would not be gainsaid, and the expeditionary force had to go along with this break from active service.

The pilgrimage to Siwa became a narrative set piece for the Alexander historians. They made out that it was a direct march across the desert, by implication through the Qattara depression, but in fact Alexander must have followed the coast road to Mersah Matruh (Paraetonium) and struck inland from there. Most of them recounted – from Callisthenes – that the party was shown the way by a group of crows (not an unlikely possibility, as the birds, too, would be drawn to the water of the oasis); Ptolemy improved on this by stating that the party was led by two talking snakes. Diodorus (Diod. Sic. 17.50.6) gives a vivid description of the oasis, some fifty *stades* (six miles) across, with a magical Spring of the Sun which became cold in the day and warmed up at night. 'The image of the god is encrusted with emeralds and other precious stones, and answers those who consult the oracle in a quite peculiar fashion. It is carried about upon a golden boat by eighty priests, and these, with the god on their shoulders, go without their own volition wherever the god directs their path.'

The actual details of the interview between Alexander and the high priest are reported in widely differing ways. Plutarch, Diodorus, Justin and Curtius all follow Cleitarchus. Callisthenes asserted that Alexander was hailed as son of Zeus. Plutarch and the Vulgate regard Alexander as having been hailed as 'son of Ammon' – which he officially was, as pharaoh. If Alexander had not undergone a coronation ceremony in Memphis, such a designation must have been a surprise, and one that made him reflect on his 'divine' status.

This episode raises the large question of Alexander's own view of his relationship to the god. To Greeks (and Macedonians) Ammon was a byname of Zeus. From here on, Alexander's devotion to Ammon is patent: he sacrifices to him regularly, he wishes to be buried in his shrine (Diod. Sic.18.2.5, Curt.10.5.4,

Just.12.15.7). But did he regard himself as actually his son? He regularly reacted with anger to taunts about his 'divine father Ammon': one of Philotas' objections to Alexander's behaviour was this claim (p.54); Cleitus' taunting of Alexander on this matter led to his murder (p. 58); and the mutineers at Opis also mocked Alexander with divine parentage, which led to the execution of several (p. 79). Bosworth (1977) has argued that his anger stemmed from a refusal to disown his father Philip, and that his claim was to dual (divine and human) parentage, like heroes such as Heracles and the Disocuri. According to Ephippus, Alexander was crowned as son of Ammon at Ecbatana in 324. In the end, the evidence is contradictory, though the balance of probability seems to be that he did regard himself as son of Ammon (why would the taunts have been made if he had given no cause for them, and why should he mind them if he did not take the idea seriously?). The question will be revisited in the discussion of the alleged deification of Alexander (Chapter 8).

Diodorus says that Alexander also, in addition to the questions detailed above, enquired whether he would rule the whole earth, and received an affirmative reply. The final question, on which all sources agree, was whether the murderers of his father had all been punished: again, the reply was affirmative, thus relieving Alexander of anxiety that he might have been remiss, as well as of the suspicion – perhaps – that his own mother had had a hand in it.

From Siwa, Alexander's party returned via the same route across the desert, and then along the coast road to Lake Mareotis. The *Romance* makes plain that he travelled by Paraetonium by providing a story which explains the name of the place (an archer's arrow, shot at a hind, went 'wide of the mark'). Shortly after passing the promontory of Taphosirion, he identified the location in which he wished to build his city. It was built in the shape of a Macedonian military cloak, on an axial grid system, and laid out by the architect Deinochares. Alexander marked out the line of the city walls with barley-meal. Birds flew down and pecked up the grain – a fact which was at first taken as a bad omen until the official seer, Aristander, leaped into the breach by announcing that the omen signified that the city would be a mother and rich in resources to numerous people. The official foundation-date of the city was 7

41

April 331. The *Romance* goes into great detail about the layout of the streets and quarters of the city. Unfortunately, none of the layout of the original city can be traced as the modern city of Alexandria lies on top of it; but some fragments of the superstructure of the great lighthouse, the Pharos, have recently been recovered from the sea near the port. (The Pharos was in fact built by Ptolemy, though later legend attributed it to Alexander.)

Alexandria was the first of many cities founded by Alexander. The *Romance* and other sources list, variously, twenty or more cities named Alexandria, and Plutarch (Plut. *de fort. Alex* 328e) claims over seventy. A recent study by P. M. Fraser (1996) has shown that many of these are in fact foundations by the Seleucid kings who followed Alexander, and named for him; others are invention; and only a few in central Asia may be taken as certain foundations by Alexander (see below, p. 57). In addition, Alexandria in Egypt is the only city which ever provides an 'ethnic' attached to a personal name (in the form 'X of Alexandria').

The foundation of a city was first of all a way of providing for superannuated troops. Such a city would act as an administrative and economic focus for its region. It would consist of a 'synoecism' of local with Greek and Macedonian settlers. It would be fortified, it would probably contain a military garrison, and it might contain such Greek amenities as a gymnasium and a theatre. Alexandria was a spectacularly successful foundation, and grew into one of the great cities of the ancient (and for that matter the modern) world.

Alexander now left Egypt behind him and returned to Tyre. Throughout the visit to Egypt, Darius had been mustering forces for a third phase of all-out war. Chief among his allies were the Bactrians under their satrap Bessus; and a new armament was a force of 200 scythed chariots. Alexander must have known what was awaiting him as he marched further into the Persian Empire.

From Greece there was more disturbing news concerning a revolt planned by King Agis of Sparta. Athens, fortunately, had declined to contribute ships; but many of the islands were now in revolt, and Agis had won control of Crete. Alexander dispatched a naval force under Amphoterus to handle the situation; but the further east he went, the less important Greek affairs became to him. All this could, and must, be left to Antipater. In fact the revolt of Agis was suppressed by the end of autumn 331; but Alexander's neglect of that small country on his western borders was to result in considerable misery for the Greek cities before his career was over.

In early summer 331, Alexander crossed the Euphrates at Thapsacus (which has never been securely identified) into territory which was still indisputably Persian. The war was on again.

6

The conquest of Persia

Alexander's army crossed the Euphrates in the high summer of 331 (probably mid-July). Alexander's objective was Babylon, but how was he to approach it? One possibility was to march directly down the Euphrates through the Mesopotamian plain, which reaches temperatures in the 40s centigrade in the summer, and is arid and short of food-supplies. There are some signs that this is what Darius expected. The satrap Mazaeus advanced up the Euphrates close to Alexander's army, and then retreated burning the land as he went, which would make Alexander's advance more difficult. Peter Green suggests that Darius was expecting Alexander to repeat the tactics of Cyrus the Younger, who had marched down the Euphrates for Babylon in 401 and won the battle of Cunaxa but had been killed in the process. If that is so, Mazaeus' actions made such a move more difficult. Instead, Alexander moved northwards and eastwards, skirting the mountains of Armenia, and arrived at the Tigris near Mosul. He spent several weeks on this journey of a mere 500 kilometres, which could have been done in a fortnight. As he arrived, there was a total eclipse of the moon, which Arrian tells us prompted him to sacrifice to Sun, Moon and Earth; Aristander the seer interpreted the eclipse as an omen favourable to Alexander.

Meanwhile Darius, even if he had not intended to force this move, had learned of Alexander's direction, and had moved into position at a spot known as Gaugamela ('camel-stall') near the city of Arbela. Incredibly, he did not oppose Alexander's crossing of the Tigris, which was easy to ford in this September season, preferring to reserve his massed cavalry strength for a pitched battle on his chosen terrain. For the third time Alexander had to fight on a battlefield chosen by the enemy, and this time it was ideal for the Persians – a wide plain with plenty of scope for cavalry and chariot movement. Darius' cavalry outnumbered Alexander's by some five to one, even though Alexander's total force now amounted to some 47,000 troops, of whom some 7000 were cavalry.

It is here that the Vulgate authors place the second offer of terms by Darius (see p. 37 above), prompted by the news that his wife had just died in captivity, and Alexander's rejection of the advice of Parmenio to accept them and return to Macedonia.

Parmenio's advice on this occasion (Arr. *Anab.* 3.10.1–2) was that, in the face of such superior forces, the only hope of success was a surprise night attack. Alexander's contemptuous response was that he 'would not steal a victory'. After working out his strategy, he slept soundly in anticipation of a battle which would go his way. Battle was joined on 30 September or 1 October. The sources go into some detail about the action – according to Aristobulus, the Persian 'order of battle' fell into Alexander's hands after the event – but what actually happened is impossible to establish with precision, and was impossible on the day, on account of the enormous amount of dust raised by the clash of armies in this desert terrain.

The Persians had chosen their position. Alexander's aim was to draw the cavalry away from the centre and enable a deep strike at that weakened point. This he in due course achieved, not least because of the inflexibility of the massed Persian troops, and the fact that their scythed chariots could not approach the sarissas of a solid phalanx. In due course the Companion Cavalry (to be distinguished from the élite Companions of the king) charged into the centre, breaking contact between Darius and Bessus, his second-in-command; then, as at Issus, the king turned tail and fled. Alexander began pursuit, but had to call it off to send help to his hard-pressed left wing. Soon, however, the defence collapsed. The field was Alexander's, along with 4000 talents of coin in the Persian tents. Darius, however, had escaped again.

Alexander could now reasonably proclaim himself ruler of the

Persian Empire. But he still had to find Darius and formally dispose of him. However, there was no need to do this instantly. The road to Babylon lay open before him. Before October was over he had received the surrender of Mazaeus and entered to the chanting of priests through the Ishtar Gate. The policy of control he developed from this stage of the campaign onwards was, in one way, a natural continuation of that he had employed hitherto, but in another way it represented an 'orientalising' tendency in his rule. Mazaeus was confirmed as satrap of Babylon, owing allegiance now to Alexander and not to Darius – though a separate Macedonian finance officer and garrison commander were appointed, as at Sardis. In many other conquered cities Alexander had left the existing rulers and governors in position; but now he confirmed in office, or selected new, rulers from the Persian nobility, the people he had come to conquer. It becomes clear that Alexander was turning himself into King of Persia, leaving his Macedonian roots far behind. So far beyond the limits of the Greek world, customs were very different and a plausible king had to behave differently in Babylonia and Iran from a Macedonian 'first among equals'. This was to become a problem later on. Garrisons, however, remained Macedonian, with Macedonian officers; and finance, too, was generally in the hands of Macedonians. In Babylon, Harpalus quickly took over control of the mint from Mazaeus. It appears that Macedonians did not on the whole learn to speak Persian; Peucestas, who was appointed governor of Persis, is singled out for mention as having done so (Arr. *Anab.* 6.30.3, 7.6.3). One or two Greeks are known to have done so (e.g. Laomedon), but the practice may well not have been general. At the same time, Alexander developed a considerable interest in Babylonian religion, and now regularly took the advice of the Chaldaean priests.

After a month's stay in Babylon, Alexander moved to Susa, the second capital of the Persian Empire, which lay in a sweltering plain near the Persian Gulf. He reached it in mid-December 331, and the satrap of Susiana, Abulites, welcomed him in without opposition, and was confirmed in office, alongside a Macedonian garrison commander and general. The wealth of Susa included not only 40,000 to 50,000 talents of gold and silver bullion, plus 9000 talents of gold coin, which Abulites at once made over to Alexander, but also considerable quantities of Xerxes' loot from Greece, including the statues of the tyrannicides, Harmodius and Aristogiton (today safely back in the National Museum in Athens).

This recovery of national treasure, and its return to Greece, should have done something to assure the Greek and Macedonian troops that the righting of Persian wrongs was still part of the agenda. They were becoming disenchanted with the seemingly endless advance, and to stifle disaffection Alexander now undertook a radical reorganisation of the army, with all territorially based groups broken up and promotion now determined purely by merit and not by seniority. Later, in spring 329, the cavalry were similarly reorganised into new units called hipparchies. Diodorus emphasises that the primary purpose of this reorganisation was to enhance the loyalty of the army, and only secondarily to improve its efficiency.

The satrap of Media, Oxydates, was found at Susa under sentence of death imposed by Darius for some unspecified crime. Alexander had him freed and reinstated as satrap of Media, thus ensuring his grateful loyalty. That loyalty seems to have wavered, however, and in 329 he was replaced by Atropates. Further east, the same principle was applied in other satrapies.

Around the beginning of January, Alexander crossed the pass from Susa to the plain of Persepolis, the Persian ceremonial capital. Resistance came both from a mountain tribe known as the Uxii, who were in the habit of extracting tolls from passing travellers, and from a fresh army collected by Ariobarzanes, the satrap of Persis; but, once these were disposed of, the governor of Persepolis, Tiridates, was willing to surrender. Phrasaortes was appointed as the new satrap of Persis; but there was a strong garrison, too. The immense wealth of Persepolis – estimated in the Vulgate as 120,000 talents – was gathered up and sent in large part to Susa, though some was reserved for the onward march of the army. The treasure included the famous 'Golden Vine' of the Persian kings, described by Herodotus. Nothing remained at Persepolis.

Near the city Alexander came upon a deputation of Greeks. These proved to be mercenaries – some 800 in total – who had been captured in battle on some uncertain occasion and had, to a man, been horribly mutilated by the loss of ears and noses, or hands, and been branded on the forehead. Here again was a chapter in the 'liberation of the Greeks'. Alexander offered to repatriate them all; but they claimed to be ashamed to return to their own kind in their hideous state, and opted rather to receive the necessary handouts to sustain themselves as farmers in the region with which they had become familiar.

Alexander now settled in to spend the winter months in the winter capital of the empire. He visited Pasargadae and the tomb of Cyrus the Great, but why did he stay so long? It may be that he was waiting to hear the outcome of the revolt of Agis; and it seems clear that he felt no urgency about the pursuit of Darius; but Peter Green's suggestion is an attractive one – that he intended to wait in Persepolis until the time of the New Year festival in April, in order to carry out the royal duties at this, the most important event of the Persian religious year.

It must, however, be admitted that our sources make no mention of his interest in this festival (except the *Alexander Romance*). In fact Alexander remained until May, and it was then that a tremendous celebration took place, at which huge quantities of unmixed wine were drunk. (Wine was a major social adhesive of the Macedonian aristocracy.) By the end of the evening, the whole of the ceremonial hall of Persepolis was aflame; the wooden columns burned readily, and the stone pillars which still stand are fissured as a result of the heat generated that night.

Was this an act of policy or a drunken outrage? The Cleitarchan tradition (the basis of Curtius, Diodorus and Plutarch) attributes the motivation to a Greek courtesan, Thais, who egged on the king to an act of destructive revenge. Even if the burning was in some sense an act of policy, it was certainly a mistaken one (as even Arrian admits), both from the point of view of winning over the Persians and from that of posterity.

By this time news had reached him that Darius was in the region of Ecbatana (Hamadan). It was time to set out in pursuit and force an issue to the troublesome question of who ruled Persia. Reinforcements reached Alexander from Greece, and it was believed that Darius was also assembling new troops and that a further pitched battle might be anticipated in northern Iran. However, on arrival in Ecbatana, Alexander was met by a Persian deserter who told him that Darius, whose new troops had not turned up, was now in retreat towards Bactria via the Caspian Gates, the pass leading between the Elburz Mountains and the northern salt desert into the eastern satrapy of Parthyene.

Instead of hastening in pursuit, Alexander remained in Ecbatana to reorganise his forces. Recognising that the crusade against Persia was effectively over, Alexander demobilised the troops of the Hellenic League with a generous bounty of one talent in addition to their pay. At the same time he offered all of them the chance to enlist with him as soldiers of fortune for the remainder of the expedition, with an initial bounty of three talents. It was clear that the expedition was moving into a new phase – of conquest for its own sake and for the sake of exploration and discovery. Alexander's *pothos* was coming into its own.

Another change was marked by the decision to leave Parmenio, now 70 years old, behind in Ecbatana as military commander. He had the task of subduing the tribes of the Caspian region, but his power was inevitably diminished. Nevertheless, his sons Philotas and Nicanor retained positions in Alexander's high command.

There were a number of new appointments in Alexander's high command at this stage (Heckel 1992, 3). They included Coenus, who accompanied Alexander to the Caspian Gates and died at the Hydaspes; Hephaestion, Alexander's long-standing and devoted friend, who had become an important though unofficial wielder of influence since Issus; Leonnatus, who received his first command now; Perdiccas, who was close to Alexander at the Persian Gates in 330; and Craterus, a loyal and patriotic Macedonian who was often at odds with Hephaestion. Some of these (Hephaestion, Leonnatus and Perdiccas) were appointed to the ranks of Alexander's official bodyguard; others who received this rank at the same time were Ptolemy (the historian, and future king of Egypt), Menes and Peucestas. Ptolemy had been a boyhood friend of Alexander, and the same was true of the elusive Harpalus (probably by now ensconced in Babylon: see Chapter 8) and Nearchus, who was later to command the fleet that returned from India to Babylon. The bodyguards all owed loyalty more to Alexander than to Macedon; and the same was true of the Pages (younger members of the Macedonian nobility, who also had the function of bodyguards), who soon came to play a more prominent role in the story.

The first stage of the pursuit of Darius took Alexander the 200 miles from Hamadan to Rhagae (Rayy, Rey), allegedly in eleven days in the heat of July. By then Darius had passed through the Gates and was on his way to Hecatompylus, later to be the summer capital of the Parthian Empire. But along the way two of his nobles, Bessus (the satrap of Bactria, which corresponds to northern Afghanistan) and Nabarzanes (the grand vizier), had lost patience with the continued retreat, deposed Darius, bound him in fetters of gold and placed him in a wagon. Bessus declared himself king, under the name of Artaxerxes IV. A group of deserters came to Alexander to show him a short cut to hasten his pursuit. Eventually Alexander came within grasping distance of the Persian force. The latter, seeing the dust of his pursuit, urged Darius to mount a horse and join them as they fled. Darius, according to Curtius (Curt. 5.13.16), 'declared that the gods had come to avenge him and, calling for Alexander's protection, refused to go along with the traitors'. Bessus and his men promptly ran Darius through with their spears and left him for dead in his wagon, being dragged wherever the beasts chose to go. In due course they came to a water-hole, and here Alexander's party caught up with the dying king.

All our sources except Arrian make a moving set piece of this final encounter of the past and future kings of Persia. (Arrian insists that Darius was dead by the time Alexander reached him.) Curtius' account is broken by a considerable lacuna; but Plutarch, Justin and the *Romance* all have Alexander weep at the fall of his foe, and Darius bequeath the kingdom to him as an honourable successor. Such a version suited Alexander's propaganda, but there could be no doubt who now had the best claim to rule of the empire. Bessus could be treated simply as a usurper; Alexander had won his throne by right of conquest.

It was late July, and Alexander lost no time in setting off in pursuit of Bessus, who had established his royal court in Bactria. It was to be nearly a year before he received his surrender.

He began by marching on Zadracarta (Sari), the capital of Hyrcania, where he received the submission of a number of Persian nobles, including Artabazus, as well as a letter from Nabarzanes asking for a safe-conduct in return for his defection. Some 1500 Greek mercenaries also sued for terms, but Alexander insisted on outright surrender from these 'criminals'.

Another alleged high-ranking visitor was Thalestris, the queen of the Amazons, the legendary race of warrior women who were usually located in the region immediately beyond the south-east corner of the Black Sea, by the River Thermodon. All the Vulgate authors, and also Strabo (11.5.4, quoting Cleitarchus for the detail that she came specifically to have a child by Alexander), include this story, which casts an interesting light on the geographical perceptions of the region by Alexander's staff as well as on Cleitarchus' capacity for myth-making. The latter element was crushingly deflated by Lysimachus who, on hearing Cleitarchus recite his account of Thalestris' thirteen-day dalliance with Alexander, asked: 'Where was I at the time?'

The geographical confusion shows clearly that the lands beyond the Caspian Sea were readily confused with those beyond the Black Sea. The eastern world was conceived by contemporary geographers as being divided by a continuous east–west line of mountains incorporating the Taurus, the Caucasus and the Hindu Kush. The Hindu Kush was generally referred to as the Caucasus. The Caspian Sea was not known to be a sea but was thought to be a gulf of the northern Ocean. The entire region of central Asia was thus telescoped and twisted around. India was thought to lie due east and to face on to the eastern Ocean. Aristotle thought that Ocean could in fact be descried from the summit of the Hindu Kush. The size of India and the very existence of China were unknown. The geography of these regions, which were little explored, remained very hazy to the end of antiquity, as a glance at a map like the Peutinger Table will show. It is possible that Alexander's staff had a picture of the Far East not unlike that represented by the medieval Mappae Mundi, with the Mediterranean at the centre, and strange races and beasts beyond the 'Caucasus' and the Caspian Gates. It was here that the land of wonders began. Alexander's own writers, like Onesicritus, made moderately sober records of what they actually did see in the distant east; but these quickly became absorbed into the exotic perceptions which went to make up the *Alexander Romance*. When the legend of Alexander became Christianised, it was easy to fit his adventures on to a map which showed Jerusalem at the centre, and to envisage him passing through lands of wonders towards the earthly paradise which lay on the outer margin of Ocean. So the geographical confusion of the ancients played a significant part in the establishment of the heroic medieval Alexander.

This stage of Alexander's expedition coincides with a marked change in his own personal habits and manner of rule. One early symptom of this was the arrival of Nabarzanes with numerous costly gifts, not least a beautiful eunuch named Bagoas. (The only source for the existence of this person, about whom Mary Renault wrote an entire novel, is a paragraph in Curtius (Curt. 6.5.22–3); Tarn, shocked at this evidence of Alexander's 'homosexuality', tried to argue Bagoas out of existence as a slanderous invention of the 'Peripatetic school' of philosophers (see p. 97 below); but Badian 1958 effectively demolished Tarn's mode of reasoning, and there is no need to dispute his existence.) Though Alexander had had a mistress for some years, same-sex relationships were always of equal importance to Greek and Macedonian aristocrats. His friendship with Hephaestion was and remained close and intense; but the sensual indulgence represented by Bagoas marked a new development in his personality. Little would now be refused Alexander, and where a modern might think of him in terms of a 'spoiled child' ancients spoke of the 'corruption' of his character by an excess of 'good fortune'. It was not hard for Alexander to believe that the gods were on his side and that he was invincible and even omnipotent.

This perception went, however, with an increasing paranoia and absoluteness in his demands for loyalty. He also found that it was necessary to act somewhat differently to make the proper impression on his Persian subjects: oriental dress, concubines, the use of two seals – one his own and one that of Darius – and the imposition of Persian cloaks on the Companions all made him an oriental king but, by the same token, alienated the Macedonians and Greeks, with their pride in their rugged simplicities. The god was becoming lonely.

Alexander's route to Bactria looks on the map like an immense detour; but a direct march on Bactra would be impossible as it would pass through the Kara Kum desert. So Alexander looped south from Hecatompylus to Herat and Kandahar, whence he could follow the lowland passes to Kabul where the crossing of the Hindu Kush from south to north was narrowest. But soon after he had passed Herat the local satrap, Satibarzanes, who had submitted to him peacefully, revolted, and Alexander had to turn back to crush the revolt. To mark the finality of the suppression, Alexander replaced Satibarzanes with another Persian, Arsaces, and founded a new city, Alexandria-in-Areia (Herat), as a focus for the control of the territory. Then Barsaentes, satrap of Drangiana (Seistan), rose in revolt. A huge backtracking into the desert borders of Iran and Afghanistan was required; Barsaentes fled to the Indus region, but the local people seized him and sent him to Alexander for execution. Satibarzanes returned and invaded Areia with the support of other satraps, but by this time Alexander was on his way to Bactria and it was left to his commander Erigyius, with the help of Artabazus, to finish off Satibarzanes. His head was delivered to Alexander in Bactra in summer 329.

But before Alexander had left the Drangian capital of Phrada (Farah) in autumn 330 one of the most important political crises of his reign had taken place.

The so-called conspiracy of Philotas is treated very briefly by Arrian on the basis of the accounts of Aristobulus and Ptolemy (who say that it had been brewing since the visit to Egypt), but is given the full rhetorical treatment with courtroom speeches by Curtius. It was the latter treatment that became classic and formed the basis of Alexander-works as diverse as the medieval German *Alexandreis* of Rudolf von Ems, Samuel Daniel's *Tragedy of Philotas* of 1605, and Terence Rattigan's play about Alexander, *Adventure Story*. No doubt this is because it encapsulates in naked form the dilemmas of autocracy and dissent, and the atmosphere of suspicion and mistrust which in a dictatorial polity prevents truth from ever being known. Certainly it cannot be known to us, though the episode may reasonably be seen as a first outrider of what Badian has termed the later 'reign of terror' exercised by Alexander. What our sources (principally Curtius and Arrian) tell us is as follows.

It began with a young man named Cebalinus. This young man's lover, Dymnus, had invited him to join a plot against Alexander's life. Cebalinus would have no part of it, and reported the story immediately to Philotas, who had just returned to Phrada from attending to the funeral of his brother Nicanor, who had died of illness in western Drangiana. Philotas promised to inform Alexander, but evidently did not think the accusations worth taking very seriously. Days passed, and he made no mention of the alleged plot to Alexander. Cebalinus grew anxious and reported the matter again, to one of the royal pages. This man took him seriously and led Cebalinus straight to Alexander, who was in the bath at the time. Alexander was enraged at the delay caused by Philotas. He had Dymnus brought to him right away. But Dymnus had fallen on his sword as soon as arrested and was unable to answer the question Alexander put to him: 'What great wrong have I planned against you, that you should think Philotas more worthy of rule than I am myself?' (Curt. 6.7.29). Alexander had plainly convinced himself of Philotas' complicity in the plot which he had so casually covered up; or he had an excuse to rid himself of a member of a family which had always represented a brake on his ambitions. Philotas was in any case not well liked: arrogant and rude, constantly making caustic remarks about Alexander's self-glorification, he had earned himself a rebuke of some kind.

Philotas was promptly arrested, together with other conspirators named by Cebalinus. An assembly was called to carry out the treason trial. Philotas spoke in his own defence, and Alexander taunted him for his refusal to speak 'in Macedonian' – a puzzling accusation which may refer to Philotas' highfalutin ways and refusal to muck in with the troops. The conclusion was foregone, but a confession was required. Philotas was taken off for torture. He at once made the confession that was expected, but was tortured anyway. In despair, he cried out to Craterus, who was in charge of the arrangements; 'Tell me what it is you want me to say.' After further torture, he was unguarded enough to point out that his father (Parmenio) controlled considerable military strength and financial resources, which Philotas would need if his plot was to be successful, and he claimed that he had hastened to carry out the plot before his elderly father died and left Philotas unable to secure these resources. He insisted, however, that his father had no part in the plot.

After this 'confession', Demetrius, another of the accused, was brought in and professed himself willing to endure torture to prove his innocence. But Philotas now addressed one Calis and said: 'Are you going to permit Demetrius to lie and me to be tortured again?' Calis had so far not fallen under suspicion, but he now confessed that he and Demetrius had together planned the crime.

Without further ado the conspirators were taken off and put to death – by stoning, the traditional Macedonian punishment for treason, according to Curtius; by being run through with javelins, according to Arrian. Though none had implicated Parmenio in any way, Macedonian tradition required the killing of the relatives of conspirators. Alexander dispatched an envoy, Polydamas, accompanied by one Cleander, to Ecbatana, carrying a letter from himself and another purportedly from Philotas. As the old man opened the letter from his son, Cleander stabbed him to death.

Tarn treated the whole episode as one in which Alexander acted without reproach throughout. Badian in 1960 by contrast argued that the conspiracy of Philotas should rather be called, as Plutarch calls it, a conspiracy *against* Philotas. The other courtiers, including Craterus, had reasons for wishing to incriminate and remove a powerful rival. Alexander himself, in Badian's view, was anxious to extricate himself 'from the stranglehold of Parmenio's family and adherents' (329). As soon as Parmenio was out of the way in Ecbatana, the plot against Philotas could be hatched, and used as an excuse to eliminate the old man also.

A final judgement is impossible. There are no doubt levels of truth, and levels of involvement in conspiracy. There probably was a plot; it is perhaps possible that Philotas was involved; it seems fairly likely that the ever-loyal Parmenio was not. But from the remote elevation of his godlike rule Alexander either could not discern the difference, or did not care; he needed absolute loyalty and support, and would stop at nothing to get it.

The one task that remained to Alexander to complete his conquest of Persia was the capture of Bessus. The satrap had retreated to Aornus in his territory of Bactria to await Alexander, who now advanced from Phrada to Kandahar. Alexander then outflanked Bessus by crossing the Hindu Kush by a high snowbound pass some eighty miles to the east. Bessus now fell back on the region of Sogdiana, in the steppe country beyond the River Oxus (Amu Darya), now the marches of Uzbekistan and Tadjikistan. Alexander occupied Aornus (Tashkurgan) and the ancient city of Zariaspa, or Bactra (Balkh), the capital of Bactria. The march to the Oxus across a blazing desert followed a mountain crossing where many had suffered frostbite; and at the end of it many of Alexander's veterans, and the Thessalian troops, insisted on being demobilised and returned home. The crossing of the Oxus took five days as the men's only means of crossing was to make floats out of their tent-covers; but they met with no opposition.

When the news of the river crossing reached Sogdiana the local satrap, Spitamenes, decided that further resistance to Alexander would be futile. His men placed Bessus under arrest and sent a message to Alexander offering to hand him over. Ptolemy was sent to receive more details, and found Bessus under armed guard in a remote village. The instructions he gave were that Bessus was to be left alone, naked, tied to a post by the road where Alexander would pass. When Alexander came upon him, he publicly questioned him as to why he had murdered his own king. His treason could not be forgiven, and Bessus was sent to Zariaspa for trial the following year (329). The Achaemenid punishment of mutilation was meted out (his nose and ears were cut off) and some time later he was executed in Ecbatana (the sources vary between crucifixion and dismemberment).

The *Alexander Romance* inserts at this point in the story a decree of Alexander to all the cities of Persia, promising the continuance of the former taxes and religious observances. While no reliable source offers a similar statement, the episode emphasises that this is the point at which Alexander is now incontrovertibly ruler of the Persian Empire, successor to the Achaemenid kings. Persian satraps continued to be appointed in Iranian provinces (Bosworth 1988, 237 ff.); while in the wilder regions of Bactria and Sogdiana military colonies of Greco-Macedonians were installed as a ruling élite. It is worth noting, too, that Alexander's coinage in the east does not continue the pattern of his Attic-standard tetradrachms in the west. In fact, no Persian Alexander coins are known, so that all his coinage must have been in the form of darics, emphasising the continuity with the former regime.

Now Alexander set off even further north to Maracanda (Samarkand). No doubt he did not entirely trust Spitamenes' submission; and he was right not to, for, on being invited to a meeting at Zariaspa, Spitamenes laid siege to Maracanda and the garrison at Zariaspa was murdered. Fierce reprisals enabled Alexander to retake the towns, and he pushed as far north as he was ever to go, to the River Jaxartes. Here he founded a city,

Alexandria Eschate (Alexandria-the-furthest), later to become Khojend.

This was the first of a network of several cities he founded north of the Oxus (six according to Curtius 7.10.15): this one was a fully fledged Greek city, complete with gymnasium and theatre (Bosworth 1988, 248). These unnamed cities seem not to have lasted long and may have been little more than military outposts. The cities attributed to Alexander in Bactria and Sogdiana are Alexandria-in-Ariana (Herat), Alexandria-in-Margiana (Merv), Alexandria Rambakia (Las Bela), Alexandria-in-Arachosia (Kandahar) and Alexandria ad Caucasum (near Begram). Ai Khanum (perhaps Alexandria-in-Oxiana) may be another. All these are south of the Oxus, and all were on the site of existing Achaemenid fortresses, and probably also had the function of aiding trade and communications. They were not, as Tarn believed, to be outposts of Greek civilisation, though they may incidentally have had such an effect, as the later development of Bactrian art suggests: see Chapter 9, p.96. (Fraser 1996, 180–2.)

Spitamenes retreated into the steppe where he could not well be pursued. It was not until late 328, when winter had already begun, that the nomad Massagetae, hearing that Alexander was again pursuing them into the steppe, decided to murder Spitamenes and brought his head to Alexander.

The intervening period, while the army was encamped at Maracanda, was full of tension. Some time was whiled away with a massive hunting expedition in which, as Bosworth puts it, 'wild game left undisturbed for generations was slaughtered *en masse*'. The hunt became famous for Alexander's killing of a lion single-handed. According to Curtius, more than 4000 beasts were slaughtered in all – an interesting sidelight on the recreational pursuits of the Macedonian aristocracy.

Another interesting sidelight on Macedonian habits is given by a much more important event, a tremendous drinking party which was held at Maracanda on the eve of the departure of the newly appointed satrap of Bactria, Cleitus the son of Dropides, who was to succeed the ageing Artabazus. The drinking was prolonged. Some flatterers in the company began to compare Alexander's achievements favourably with those of Castor and Pollux, the sons of Zeus, and 'others did not even leave Heracles untouched'. This flattery touched a raw nerve in Cleitus; he had made it plain for some time that he was aggrieved both by Alexander's change-over to the more barbaric style and by the expressions of his flatterers; and now under the stimulus of wine he would not let them show disrespect for the divine power, or belittle the deeds of the heroes of old, to do Alexander a favour that was none. Nor in his view were Alexander's achievements so great and wonderful as they cried them up to be; and Alexander had not achieved them by himself, but they were in great part Macedonian achievements. Alexander was deeply hurt by his words.

(Arr. *Anab.* 4.8.4–5)

Arrian went on to register his own disapproval of this speech: courtiers should know how to keep their opinions to themselves. But Cleitus was now in full flood; he began to boast of his own achievement in saving Alexander from death at the Granicus, until at last Alexander called for the hypaspists to take him away. The order was ignored. What happened next is reported differently in the various accounts, but the upshot was that Alexander seized a spear, perhaps from one of the bodyguards, and thrust it straight into Cleitus' chest, killing him instantly.

Alexander was filled with remorse and was on the verge of throwing himself on the same lance to kill himself, but was restrained. He then retired to his room and remained there for three days, refusing food and water and crying out the names of Cleitus and of his sister Hellanice, who had nursed him. This Homeric bout of mourning was brought to an end by the blandishments of Anaxarchus, one of the philosophers who travelled with the court. He talked Alexander out of his distress by arguing that whatever a king does is just, and that therefore Alexander should not blame himself. If this report is true, it must have been – as it certainly was for the ancient historians – a further stage in the moral decline of the king.

Anaxarchus of Abdera seems to have been a regular rival of the other philosopher at Alexander's court, Callisthenes of Olynthus, the official historian (Borza 1981). Possibly at odds philosophically – Callisthenes, the nephew of Aristotle, being presumably an Aristotelian Anaxarchus probably a sceptic – as well as in their personal habits – luxurious in the case of Anaxarchus, austere in that of Callisthenes – the two men became even more polarised after this event. The trouble with

Callisthenes came to a head as a result of Alexander's increasing adoption of Persian ways, dress and ceremonial – in particular his insistence on *proskynesis* or obeisance. The precise nature of the behaviour demanded has been much discussed; the Greek word means something like 'blowing a kiss', and has been compared with Persian reliefs which show officials bending forward slightly, fingers to lips, to honour a king or deity. However, it seems that the same term was used, from Herodotus onwards, for the complete prostration of a subject before the king (1.134). Such an act was undignified and abhorrent for Greeks, who used the term *proskynesis* to describe an attitude of prayer before gods only: it was not appropriate for free men to abase themselves before other men.

The practice became bound up with the movement to acknowledge Alexander as a god, which as we have seen was common talk among his flatterers. The discussion was brought much further on one occasion by Anaxarchus, who proposed that

> there was no doubt that when Alexander had departed from among them they would honour him as a god; how much more just, then, that they should give him his due in life rather than when he was dead and the honour would profit him nothing.

(Arr. *Anab.* 4.10.7)

This suggestion, in Arrian's account, provoked a long speech from Callisthenes arguing that it was outrageous to demand such obeisance from Greeks, which was only fit for barbarians. His speech pleased the Macedonians; but the Persians present are said to have happily adopted the habit of obeisance. On another occasion Alexander sent round a loving cup with the requirement that everyone present, after drinking from it, should pay him obeisance and then kiss him. All the Companions duly did so, but when it came to Callisthenes' turn he omitted the obeisance. The failure was pointed out to Alexander, whereupon he refused the kiss. Callisthenes said: 'Very well, then; I go away the poorer by a kiss.'

This intransigence of Callisthenes naturally diminished his standing with Alexander, and in due course led to his being implicated in the Conspiracy of the Pages. The Pages were the sons of Macedonian notables who attended the king, guarded him when asleep, and looked after the horses. One of the Pages,

Hermolaus, was said to have been incensed by an episode while hunting, when Hermolaus had struck a boar before Alexander and Alexander had ordered him to be whipped for infringing his privilege. (The story became a commonplace of history-writing, and the same motive was adduced by one historian for the murder of Odenathus of Palmyra some six centuries later.) This insult is supposed to have been enough to stir up Hermolaus and his friend to concoct a plot to kill Alexander in his sleep, which was only frustrated because on the appointed night Alexander stayed up until dawn drinking. Next day, after he had slept off his hangover, Alexander learned of the plot and had all those implicated tortured on the rack. Among those they denounced was Callisthenes, according to Aristobulus; but Arrian takes the view that Alexander was ready to find any opportunity to rid himself of Callisthenes. The Pages were executed, but Callisthenes' fate is variously told. Ptolemy said that he was tortured and hanged, but Aristobulus and Chares, the court chamberlain, wrote that he was imprisoned and carried along with the army in a kind of cage, until he became so disease-ridden and infected with lice that he died some time early in 325, in India. The fate of this philosopher was the ultimate source of the 'philosophic opposition' to Alexander which characterised the writings of Stoic and other philosophers into Roman times: Seneca (NQ 6.23.2) calls it 'Alexander's eternal shame'.

These unpleasant events concluded the stay in Central Asia, and with the spring of 327 the march into India began.

7

The expedition to India

It had been for some time part of Alexander's plan to conquer India. It was here that his *pothos*, his 'yearning', came into full play. The geographical conceptions of the time made it possible to believe that India represented the last land before the encircling Ocean, so that an invasion of India would constitute a conquest of the entire world to the east of Greece. (The west would come later.) This plan had first been made explicit when Alexander received an embassy from Pharasmanes, a king of the Chorasmians on the Oxus. (His name was later to be attached to a 'Letter to Hadrian' describing the fabulous beasts of India and the Far East.) Pharasmanes had promised help in Central Asia; and Alexander had also received an embassy from the ruler of Taxila, known as Taxiles. Both saw advantages to themselves in lending aid to Alexander's conquests.

Mythology also came into his considerations. Alexander consciously modelled his exploits on those of the gods and heroes of Greece, as well as of human predecessors such as Cyrus the Great. Dionysus was supposed to have come from India to make himself a god in Greece, with his retinue of panthers and maenads, his garlands of grapes and ivy; Alexander would retrace the god's steps to his origins. Heracles, too, had been this way. Finally, the legendary Queen Semiramis of Assyria was a constant object of emulation; she alone of western rulers had carried her conquests to India and Central Asia (Agathias,

Histories 2.25.4–5), and Alexander would imitate her. It was her example that was to lead him back through the Gedrosian Desert of south Iran, and which was to lead to legends that he had also, like her, conquered Ethiopia.

The scientific staff were primed for such an expedition. Geographical researches had already been carried out (with what accuracy we have already seen). Ethnographers and natural historians were ready to encounter beasts, plants and other phenomena as strange as those that had already been described by the fifth-century author Ctesias. These included the giant palmyra tree, the river of honey, the men with dog's heads and the men with reversed feet, as well as the monstrous manticore with its three rows of teeth. If the expedition did not find them, those who wrote it up would make sure to claim that it did. Baeton referred knowledgeably to the reverse-feet men; Cleitarchus lost no opportunity to enhance his history with wonders; and the apogee of all these stories came in the *Alexander Romance* and the 'Letter from Alexander to Aristotle' which was incorporated in it. But perhaps the most interesting of the writers on India was Onesicritus, who combined information about banyan trees and trees which bore wool on their branches with accounts of the Utopian life of the kingdom of Musicanus and a highly influential interview with some Indian ascetics at Taxila (of which more below).

The necessary military force was assembled, and the first task of the spring of 327 was the conclusion of the reduction of Sogdia with the conquest of the Sogdian Rock. Its ruler, Oxyartes, had mocked the Macedonians by telling them that they could only take it if they could find soldiers with wings; but Alexander called for volunteers for some serious mountaineering, and with the aid of ropes and iron pitons a considerable detachment made the ascent by night. The Sogdians capitulated immediately; and the completeness of their submission was indicated by the fact not only that Oxyartes was instrumental in arranging the capitulation of a second rock, of Chorienes, but also that a marriage was soon arranged between Alexander and the daughter of Oxyartes, Roxane.

Marriage was essential if Alexander was to hand his kingdom to an heir. Alexander had had a Greek mistress, Barsine (formerly the wife of Memnon of Rhodes), since 333, but marriage with its dynastic implications had not so far entered his plans.

The report (Plut. *Alex*. 30) that Darius' wife had died in childbirth is imponderable as the date of this event is uncertain. It is associated by the sources with Darius' second embassy to Alexander: this was, as we have seen, placed by Arrian in spring 332, four or five months after her capture; but if it were to be placed where the Vulgate have it, in summer 331, the putative father would surely be Alexander.

The marriage to Roxane had a political advantage in securing the Macedonians' rear; perhaps, too, Alexander's thoughts turned to the production of an heir as he began his venture into lands where no man had trodden, and from which – how could he know? – he might never return. If that is so, the conception of an heir proved no speedy event.

The army which crossed the Hindu Kush in spring 327 may have been as large as 120,000, including camp-followers of all kinds (Peter Green), and was almost certainly well in excess of the 30,000 troops estimated by Sir William Tarn.

The Macedonian element was now not more than 15,000 including 2000 cavalry. The rest were soldiers of fortune from Greece and elsewhere, and unidentified numbers of Persian and other locally conscripted troops. This army crossed the Hindu Kush by the Salang Pass in ten days (rather than by the difficult route through Bamiyan which he had used previously), arriving at the city he had founded in his earlier expedition, Alexandria-in-the-Caucasus, somewhere to the north of Kabul. From here a straightforward lowland route led to the east, crossing through the Khyber Pass into the hills of what the Victorians knew as the 'North-West Frontier' and thence into the Indus Plain.

In the Kabul valley, Alexander was already within the confines of 'India', and here he received an embassy, by pre-arrangement, from the ruler of Taxila. Taxila (Takshacila), near modern Rawalpindi, was one of the oldest and most distinguished cities of the region, a 'university city' even before the period of Achaemenid rule, and home to the famous grammarian Panini and the political scientist Kautilya. Its ruler, Ambhi (Greek Omphis), who was also known as Taxiles, hoped for Alexander's support against Porus, a rival monarch, whose kingdom lay south of the Hydaspes (Jhelum), and quickly entered into an alliance with him.

Hephaestion, with the bulk of the army and supplies, now proceeded, under Ambhi's guidance, to the Indus, while

Alexander took a detachment up the valley of the Choaspes (Kunar) into Swat to ensure the region's submission. The campaign was a difficult one; the terrain was hard going, and the tribes of the Afghan–Pakistani borderlands were ferocious fighters. Alexander reduced the cities with corresponding savagery, at one (Massaga) slaughtering 7000 of the inhabitants – an action which Plutarch regarded as one of the greatest stains on his military career.

Somewhere in this region an embassy approached Alexander asking for special consideration because of the sanctity of their city. As Arrian describes it (Arr. *Anab.* 5.1), a chieftain named Acuphis, accompanied by thirty supporters, came to Alexander in his tent and announced that this place, Nysa, was a foundation of the god Dionysus:

> for when Dionysus had subdued the nation of the Indians, and was returning towards the Greek sea, he founded this city with the men unfit for service among his soldiers, who were also his Bacchi, to be a memorial to posterity of his wanderings and victory, just as you yourself founded Alexandria by Mount Caucasus and another Alexandria in Egypt, and as there are many other cities you have founded already or will found in course of time and thus give proof of more achievements than those of Dionysus.

The story may be invention, but the Greeks at least were willing to be persuaded of the special connections with Dionysus of this place, because it was the only place they found in the region where ivy, the sacred plant of Dionysus, would grow. It would appear that the locals were able to represent their own god, perhaps Shiva, as the local name of Dionysus.

Unfortunately it is impossible to know just where this significant place was. According to Curtius (Curt. 8.10.11 ff.), it was high in the mountains in a wooded region, west of the Choaspes, by implication of its place in the narrative before Alexander reached Massaga. Arrian, however, locates Nysa 'between the Cophen [Kabul] and the Indus' (5.1.1), therefore perhaps in the region of Peshawar. Modern scholars differ, Green and Lane Fox for example placing it near Chitral and Bosworth not far from Jalalabad. The only way to answer the question might seem to be an expedition to find the ivy; another clue is the cedarwood coffins hanging in trees to which the troops accidentally set fire in the night, for Lane Fox (1973, 342) has described seeing such coffins among the Kafir people of Nuristan, who expose their dead in them.

The importance of the episode is the emphasis it lays on Alexander's divine mission, his role as a successor to Dionysus. This aspect of his self-presentation was given another encouragement when he was wounded during the attack on Massaga; one of the bystanders quoted a line from Homer, 'Ichor, such as flows from the blessed gods' (Aristobulus, *FGrHist*139F47); Alexander snapped back that the substance was blood, not ichor, but the point was made. Another divine ambition was to reduce the Rock of Aornus which even Heracles (presumably a 'translation' of Krishna, in a local legend) had failed to conquer. This massif was authoritatively identified by the great explorer Sir Aurel Stein (1929) as Pir-Sar, in a bend of the Indus 5000 feet above the river. Alexander was now close enough to Hephaestion to re-establish contact and to send for reinforcements. Alexander brought his siege catapults up the Una-Sar which faced the fortress, some 8000 feet, and constructed a ramp to bring them in range of the rock – at which point the defenders capitulated. Military supremacy coincided with another demonstration of superhuman or 'super-Heraclean' achievement. Alexander was able to advance leaving a pacified region behind him (though the Assaceni of Massaga were to revolt within the year).

In spring 326, Alexander advanced to the Indus. Here he was welcomed by Ambhi, who laid on a tremendous parade to escort the army into Taxila. Finding it for once unnecessary to fight to maintain their position, the expedition remained some three months in Taxila, and this provided an excellent opportunity for the researchers in Alexander's party to get on with their investigations. One group of people who attracted the interest of Onesicritus were the ascetics known to the Greeks as the *gymnosophistae*, or 'naked philosophers'. These aroused tremendous interest also among later writers, some of whom referred to them as Brahmans; the *Alexander Romance* created considerable confusion by identifying them with the Brahmans of the Lower Indus who were instrumental in fomenting opposition to Alexander several months later.

Aristobulus (as reported by Strabo 15.1.61) 'says that he saw two of the sophists at Taxila, both Brachmanes; and that the elder had his head shaved but that the younger had long hair; and that both were followed by disciples'. Strabo also tells us (15.1.63–5) that Onesicritus was sent to converse with these 'philosophers'. Holding such conversation as he could through the medium of not one but three interpreters (which, as he said, was like trying to get water to run clear through mud), he discovered some remarkable affinities between the ascetics' doctrines and those of the Cynic school to which he belonged. The piquant contrast between the Cynic lifestyle, which went without the most basic necessities of civilisation, and the royal state of Alexander led Arrian to narrate this episode in a special place alongside the earlier encounter of Alexander with Diogenes at Corinth. Inevitably the story grew up that Alexander had talked to them himself; Arrian says that they addressed him as follows:

> King Alexander, each man possesses no more of this earth than the patch we stand on; yet you, though a man like other men, except of course that you are restless and presumptuous, are roaming over so wide an area away from what is your own, giving no rest to yourself or to others. And very soon you too will die, and will possess no more of the earth than suffices for the burial of your body. (Arr. *Anab.* 7.1.6)

This encounter became a philosophers' set piece; a much more elaborate version occurs in Plutarch and the *Alexander Romance*, and freestanding versions of the conversation were also circulating as early as 100 BC, as papyrus finds show (Wilcken 1923). The story is perhaps the most resonant of all Alexander stories and was still being rewritten throughout the Middle Ages; the latest new version is in an English chapbook of 1683 (Stoneman 1994; 1995).

The leader of the ascetics is named as Dandamis (a word perhaps related to the Sanskrit word for a Brahman's staff); also among them was one Calanus, who was inveigled into joining Alexander's expedition as a kind of performing philosopher. He created his own spectacular anecdote when, falling ill in Persia, he committed suicide by burning himself to death on a pyre – an act which became associated with Indian philosophers for some time afterwards, and even turned into a fashion which was satirised by Lucian in his *Life of Peregrinus*.

Beguiled by such distractions, and reassured by a mission

from Abisares, the king of the region to the north-west of Taxila, Alexander delayed his advance across the Indus to meet the most dangerous of his adversaries in the Punjab: Porus ('the Paurava ruler'), whose lands lay between the Hydaspes (Jhelum) and the Acesines (Chenab). When he set out it was June, and the monsoon rains had already begun. The sources claim that he made the march of 110 miles from Taxila to the ford of the Jhelum, probably at Haranpur, in two days. But the courses of the five rivers of the Punjab have altered considerably over the centuries, and it cannot be certain exactly where the crossing and battle took place. Porus' troops were drawn up on the opposite bank of the Jhelum and amounted to some 3000–4000 cavalry and 50,000 infantry; in addition he had not only war-chariots but several war-elephants – a challenge the Macedonian army had not faced before (though Alexander had acquired a few elephants of his own as a gift from Ambhi).

Alexander's main aim, as he faced the Indian's army across the river, was to confuse his enemy as much as possible. He spent several nights arranging sorties and lighting fires at different points up and down the bank; he is also said to have changed his clothes with a Macedonian officer of similar build so that the enemy would be uncertain where the centre of command lay. Finally he identified a crossing-point, some seventeen miles up-river, where an island provided good cover for the transport-ships. The largest body of troops was brought across the river under cover of darkness and with the additional concealment of a tremendous thunderstorm, in which several men were struck by lightning. Craterus at the base camp was instructed not to attempt a crossing until the Indians were fully engaged with the attack from upstream.

Porus' chariots proved useless in the muddy terrain, but the elephants were a formidable obstacle for the Macedonians. The *Alexander Romance* invented a fabulous tale (lovingly illustrated in medieval manuscripts) of how Alexander prepared a front line of bronze warriors, who were heated to red heat and sent the elephants howling into retreat as they tried to wrap their trunks around them. In actual fact, the only stratagem could be constant harrying with spears and arrows; even then many Macedonian troops were trampled under the elephants' feet. Porus' son was killed early in the fighting. Gradually the Macedonians surrounded the Indian troops, until Porus, wounded in the shoulder, retreated from the field on the back of his huge elephant. (Shekels of Alexander, issued – perhaps from the Susa (Stewart) or Babylon (Bosworth) mint – soon after the victory, show a Macedonian horseman prodding cheekily with his lance at the rear of a retreating elephant.) Porus was captured and brought to Alexander, who in a famous exchange asked him how he expected to be treated. 'Like a king' was the dignified reply. The encounter was a memorable one, as Porus was, by all reports, a very tall man, nearly seven feet tall; Alexander will have come not far above his lower ribs. Rather than deposing him, Alexander confirmed him as ruler of his previous lands, but now as a vassal of the Macedonian king – an indication not so much of a liberal policy of rule as of Alexander's impatience with administrative arrangements which might distract him from fighting and exploration.

Alexander's horse, Bucephalas, who had accompanied him throughout the expedition, was killed in this battle. A 'city' was founded and named after the horse – Bucephala – as well as another city, Nicaea (Victory Town), where tremendous athletic contests were laid on to celebrate the victory. But Alexander was already preparing to move on. The rest of India beckoned. He quickly crossed the Acesines (Chenab) and the Hydraotes (Ravi), arriving in the region of Lahore. The local peoples submitted without a struggle, except for a short siege at Sangala (probably modern Sangla). 'He intended', says Diodorus (Diod. Sic. 17.89.4), 'to reach the borders of India and to subdue all of its inhabitants, and then to sail downstream to the Ocean.' Arrian gives Alexander a great speech to his officers after arriving at the next river, the Hyphasis (Beas), in which he made much play with the parallels of Dionysus and Heracles, and insisted that the conquest of the whole of India was necessary to ensure the safety of the lands conquered so far.

If anyone longs to hear what will be the limit of the actual fighting, he should understand that there remains no great stretch of land before us up to the river Ganges and the eastern sea. This sea, I assure you, will prove to be joined to the Hyrcanian Sea; for the great sea encircles all the land. And it will be for me to show Macedonians and allies alike that the Indian Gulf [Arabian Sea] forms but one stretch of water with the

Persian Gulf, and the Hyrcanian Sea with the Indian Gulf. From the Persian Gulf our fleet shall sail round to Libya, as far as the Pillars of Hercules [Straits of Gibraltar]; from the Pillars all the interior of Libya then becomes ours, just as Asia is in fact becoming ours in its entirety. (Arr. *Anab.* 5.26.1–2)

The sources of this speech in Arrian cannot be known, and it may be that, like many speeches in ancient historians, it is substantially the invention of the author; but it seems to reflect Alexander's intentions, and also what he believed about the geography of the world still to be traversed. A local ruler had told Alexander that it was only twelve days' march to the Ganges, a report sharply criticised by Brunt (1983, 463; app. 17.22) as 'nonsense'; but in fact the distance from the Hyphasis to the upper reaches of the Ganges is only a couple of hundred miles. The fact that the Ganges itself flows more than fifteen hundred miles to the sea is another matter!

For the officers as for the vast mass of Alexander's army, these further plans were too much. Exhausted by the unceasing rain of the monsoon – and how were they to know whether it ever stopped raining in this land? – the task of conquering Persia achieved (Achaemenid rule had never extended beyond the Hyphasis), and their mastery of Asia confirmed, they found Alexander's continuing ambition incomprehensible and his demands unreasonable. They mutinied. The officers refused to go, and so did the troops.

Alexander tried the Achilles tactic of retiring to his tent to sulk. Three days later, he was still there and the army showed no sign of changing its mind. Alexander now decided that he would mark the limit of his conquest by erecting a series of twelve altars (Curtius, Arrian), and start the return home. According to Philostratus in his *Life of Apollonius* (2.43), these altars were dedicated to Ammon, Heracles, Athena, Zeus, the Cabiri of Samothrace, Indus, Helios (the Sun) and Apollo. This weird assemblage is not confirmed by other writers, but the altars became a regular feature of ancient maps, as we can tell from their appearance on the late antique Peutinger Table (marked 'usque quo Alexander' and 'hic Alexander responsum accepit' – a reference to the legend known to us from the *Romance* in which celestial creatures admonished Alexander not to pursue his explorations further), as well as on the medieval Mappae Mundi which derive from Agrippa's world map prepared for Julius Caesar.

Alexander began to return to the Hydraotes and to prepare for a return journey which would cap anything achieved by any of his predecessors, including the legendary Semiramis. The plan now was to sail down the Indus and to return via the Indian Ocean to the Iranian heartland of his empire. To begin with, Arrian tells us, Alexander had believed that all the land to the south of him was continuous, a vast southern continent, and that the Indus flowed directly into the Nile:

> He had already seen crocodiles on the Indus, as on no other river except the Nile, and beans growing on the banks of the Acesines of the same sort as the land of Egypt produces and, having heard that the Acesines runs into the Indus, he thought he had found the origin of the Nile. (Arr. *Anab.* 6.1.2)

He reported on this, Arrian says, in a letter to his mother, but on receiving better information cancelled that passage of the letter. The status of this letter is unclear, and the implication seems to be that a copy was kept in the archives. It is not mentioned by Plutarch among the letters on which he drew for information about Alexander's march (Plutarch was not very interested in geography), and it bears no relation to the wondrous fictional letter to Olympias about his travels included in the *Alexander Romance*, on which one might expect it to have had some impact. Some of the events of the voyage that followed did find an echo in the legends of the *Romance*, and also had an impact on other fictional writing. But at the point of departure Alexander's geographical information was sound.

The army returned to the Jhelum where it was increased by reinforcements, and kitted out with 25,000 newly arrived suits of armour; the tattered equipment with which Alexander's men had come so far was burned. The fleet set off in November 326 and sailed down the River Acesines (Chenab) towards its junction with the Indus. Craterus and his troops marched down the right bank, Hephaestion with his troops down the left. The voyage did not begin peacefully, as they encountered strong resistance from two local peoples, the Malli and the Oxydracae. These peoples are the Malavas and Kshudrakas, who occur, in association with some other groupings, also in the Indian national epic, the *Mahabharata*. The battle to capture the town of the Malli was the occasion of one of the most dramatic episodes of Alexander's career. The omens were against him, and the men hung back. Alexander seized one of the scaling-ladders and swiftly ascended it, plunging over the battlements into the crowd of defenders. Three other Macedonians quickly joined him, but Alexander was cornered under a tree, taking on all comers. Before the mass of the Macedonians was able to break through into the city, Alexander was wounded in the chest by an arrow and collapsed. His companions shielded him from the onrush of Indians, and eventually he was borne away to the camp. The removal of the arrowhead caused immense loss of blood, and Alexander fainted. He remained at the point of death for a week, but his remarkably strong constitution enabled him to pull through. For the first time the possibility of his death seemed a real one; but his authority and, in fact, his indispensability to the expedition remained undinted.

This episode is the occasion of a curious and exemplary conflict in the sources. Who exactly was with Alexander on that day? Arrian, whose account I have followed, says that there were three: Peucestas, Leonnatus and Abreas. Plutarch mentions only two (perhaps not counting the obscure Abreas). Cleitarchus, however, states that Ptolemy was also with him, as does Timagenes. It is certain that he was not; if he had been, he would certainly have mentioned it in his own account, which Arrian used. What is the motive here for Cleitarchus' false information? His aim is usually supposed to be that of glorifying Alexander with extravagant achievements, but this event does not fit that pattern – a warning against being too certain of tracing any particular version of an episode to any one author. However, Cleitarchus exhibits considerable interest in Ptolemy, and was doubtless concerned to flatter a king who could give him patronage and preferment. The story has also been thought to be a factitious explanation for Ptolemy's later title of Soter, 'Saviour'.

The Malli submitted, and the Kshudrakas surrendered without a struggle. The fleet sailed on, Alexander prostrate on a day-bed on the deck, keeping some way ahead of the other ships 'so that the quiet which he still needed might not be interrupted by the beat of the oars' (Curt. 9.6.2).

Another five months of travel and constant fighting brought the army to the head of the Indus delta at Pattala (July 325). Craterus meanwhile had departed to go overland to Carmania (Kerman province in Iran) to await the arrival of the remainder of the expedition by its more circuitous route. He received submission and gifts from Musicanus, the king of the region around Sukkur, and defeated the hill tribes under the command of Sambus, whose capital was at Sindimana (near Sehwan in Sind), as well as a revolt organised by the Brahmans, advisers to the rulers, in the same region. Musicanus then revolted, and the rising was savagely quelled: Musicanus and the Brahmans were hanged. These Brahmans became gloriously confused with the Oxydracae and with the Brahmans or naked sophists of Taxila in the account of the *Alexander Romance*; but this was not the only piece of fiction inspired by this part of the expedition. Onesicritus, the historian who had been sent to interview the Taxila sophists, found here another opportunity for philosophical invention, As Strabo tells us:

> He goes on to speak of the country of Musicanus at some length, eulogizing it; some of their characteristics are shared with the rest of the Indians, like their longevity, some of them reaching the age of a hundred and thirty . . . their simple manner of living, and their healthiness. . . . A feature peculiar to them is the establishment of Spartan *syssitia* [communal dinners] . . . also the fact that they make no use of gold and silver, although they have mines . . . they do not pursue study of the sciences far, except for medicine, and indeed extended study of some sciences, such as military science and the like, is regarded as criminal; and there are no lawsuits except for homicide and assault, on the principle that it is not within a man's power to escape from being the victim of these crimes, but terms of agreement are within the control of each individual.
> (Strabo 15.1.34)

In short, the place is a Cynic Utopia. Nor was Onesicritus the only author to discover a Utopia in this region. An author called Amometus (cited by Pliny *NH* 6.54–5) wrote a *History of the Attacorae*, another people of the region, which was in effect a philosophical Utopia. In the early years of the third century the composition of Utopias, usually in the form of fictional travellers' tales, became quite popular, and this particular genre is another unexpected legacy of Alexander's epoch-making expedition.

More surprises were in store for the army south of Pattala (Hyderabad). The south-west monsoon was now blowing, and the passage was a rough one; in addition, at this point the Indus becomes tidal, and the Macedonians, used to the tideless waters of the Mediterranean, were thoroughly alarmed at finding their ships suddenly aground on mudbanks. They wandered disconsolately around them, encountering giant crabs and other unpleasant creatures destined to become the stuff of legend. They were even more alarmed when the tide rushed in and their ships suddenly floated off again.

At about this time (late summer 325) the satrapy of India revolted (Bactria and Sogdiana had already revolted at the end of 326). The leaders of this revolt were Sandrocottus, soon to achieve great fame as Chandragupta, the founder of the Maurya empire, and in association with him Porus who had been thought loyal. 'India' was slipping from Alexander's grasp even before he had left its confines; but the king's mind was now entirely on the future.

The expedition here divided into two. Nearchus was to take the fleet and sail along the coast of the Indian Ocean, while Alexander would march his troops through the desert of Gedrosia, the barren region bordering the coast and crossing the frontiers of Pakistan and Iran. His main reason for this rash enterprise was to emulate the legendary Queen Semiramis, who was supposed to have conquered India and to have returned to Babylon via this route. For once ambition outstripped reason, or his advance intelligence was badly at fault. Though the march began well, water soon became impossible to find, and no provisions could be got from the only local inhabitants they came across, a tribe still living in the Stone Age whom the Greeks called the Fish Eaters, who dressed in sharkskins and built their huts from whales' skeletons. Further inland, there were date palms, but an unremitting diet of these caused disease, and other plants turned out to be poisonous. The searing heat of the region and the lack of provisions resulted in the loss of maybe 60,000 men during the sixty-day march to Carmania.

This march is the most likely occasion of a tale of heroic action by Alexander which different authors place at different points in his career. A soldier, discovering a small pool of brackish water, scooped some up and brought it to Alexander in a helmet. Alexander, however, refused to be privileged with a gift which the whole army needed as much as he did; he poured the water out into the sand, thus setting an example of endurance to the rest. Finally at Gwadar the army picked up the road inland to Pura (Iranshahr) which would lead on to Susa. The remainder of the journey was covered in a more relaxed style, and several authors tell us that Alexander treated the march as a Bacchic procession with revelry of all kinds:

> He gave orders for villages along his route to be strewn with flowers and garlands, and for bowls full of wine and other vessels of extraordinary size to be set out on the thresholds of houses. . . . The friends and the royal company went in front, heads wreathed with various kinds of flowers woven into garlands, with the notes of the flute heard at one point, the tones of the lyre at another . . . the king and his drinking companions rode in a cart weighed down with golden bowls and huge goblets of the same metal. In this way the army spent seven days on a drunken march, an easy prey if the vanquished races had only had the courage to challenge riotous drinkers . . . but it is fortune that allots fame and a price to things, and she turned even this piece of disgraceful soldiering into a glorious achievement! (Curt. 9.10.25–27)

But it was a pitiful remnant of the army that had set out that was reunited in Carmania with Craterus.

The men who arrived with Nearchus at Susa in December were in a scarcely better state. For the first time, Alexander's arrangements for commissariat had gone seriously wrong. Nearchus, too, had his tales to tell – for example, of the island on which they beached, only to find it swim off, thus revealing itself as a whale. Curiously, exactly the same thing happened to Sindbad the sailor and to St Brendan – not to mention Baron Munchausen.

The arrival in Carmania marked the return from the wilderness to the real world, and Alexander had much work waiting for him.

8

Alexander in Babylon

Alexander's arrival back in the Iranian heartland of his empire reintroduced him to problems of administration and rule which had been put in abeyance, if not forgotten, during the expedition to India. While still in Pura he had heard of trouble with the satrap of Oreitis, Apollophanes, whom he promptly deposed. Craterus had also had to crush a revolt some way to the north of Pura. The satrap of Carmania, Astaspes, was welcomed to the celebrations for the return home; but his execution turned out to be one of the entertainments at the revel. Several other executions followed, including those of the Macedonian generals Cleander and Sitalces, accused of maladministration in Media. A little later, when Alexander arrived in Persepolis, he executed the satrap Orxines, on the grounds that he had allowed the tomb of Cyrus to be robbed, and replaced him with the loyal Peucestas, who had been one of his saviours at the town of the Malli. Peucestas, according to Diodorus (Diod. Sic. 19.14.5), was the sole satrap permitted to wear Persian dress, an indication of the importance attached to the adhesion of the inhabitants of this satrapy. These regions could not be dropped as soon as won in the way that the kingdom of Porus had been.

These acts of retribution for maladministration seem to have had an impact on one of Alexander's longest-standing administrators, Harpalus, the treasurer, based in Babylon. In spring 324 he left his post for Greece. It was not the first time he had fled at a moment of crisis, and this is a good point to survey his career and its implications.

Harpalus had been associated with Alexander since their earliest years. Some ailment made him unfit for military service, and he had become treasurer of Alexander's empire as early as 336. Shortly before the battle of Issus (November 333) he had fled his post for the first time to travel to Greece. Arrian tells us cryptically that he had become involved with an adventurer named Tauriscus, and scholars have pondered what might be the true reason for this flight. Peter Green and Lane Fox think that he may have been on some kind of spying mission; Bosworth suggests that he thought Macedon a safer place to be than Cilicia if Alexander should die of his fever caused by swimming in the Cydnus. The most obvious explanation, embezzlement, has been thought to be ruled out as Harpalus was reinstated in his post by 331. But Worthington (1984) has suggested that the two things are not incompatible. Alexander may have felt unable to dispense with his services. We are told that Alexander 'forgave' his flight – and, as is clear in the case of Cleomenes of Naucratis (pp.84–5), peculation did not worry Alexander too much as long as his own interests were protected.

At all events, Harpalus was back in post by 331, and some time thereafter, perhaps in 330, his base of operations was relocated to Babylon. Here he was in complete charge of the treasury, with all the bullion acquired by Alexander in his expedition, and was in charge of the minting of coinage for the empire (shekels for the Levant and Cilicia, darics for Iran). The possibilities for corruption were enormous; but, so far as we can tell, Harpalus at first devoted his spare time in Babylon to gardening, importing Greek plants for the royal parks, all of which flourished except ivy, which could not endure the sweltering heat. Soon, however, he also imported an expensive Athenian mistress, Pythionice, replacing her when she died with a new Athenian, Glycera.

It seems that he may have begun to mint coins also without reference to Alexander. At the least he was hedging his bets against Alexander's demise, at worst he might have been seen as preparing to revolt against Alexander, or at least to set himself up as king in Babylon.

As early as the voyage down the Indus, news of his activities had reached the army. A satyr play, *Agen* – some said Alexander was the author – was staged; it included much lampooning of Harpalus, of Glycera, 'the Queen of Babylon', and of the Athenians. When news of Alexander's crackdown on the satraps got out, Harpalus felt sufficiently threatened to decamp promptly. He made straight for Athens. Here, however, despite the generous shipments of grain and dedications of temples he had made in previous years, he was coolly received.

The Athenians also had to hedge their bets. Harpalus was put under guard, and the 700 talents he had brought with him were stored on the Acropolis. He soon escaped and rejoined his mercenaries on Crete, where he was killed by one of his subordinates. Thus came to an end the career of one of Alexander's most enigmatic associates.

His fate was entwined with important developments in Alexander's relations with mainland Greece, which began to take shape after the king's arrival at Susa in February/March 324. But Alexander's first actions on reaching Susa were also of considerable significance. The surviving Persian royal women had been left here during the expedition to India; now it was time to provide them with husbands. He did more than that. He arranged a mass marriage of himself and ninety-one other members of his court to noble Persian wives. He himself took two wives: the daughters of Darius and of Artaxerxes Ochus. Many of the marriages do not seem to have lasted, and they clearly took place under some duress; but they signalled an important change in the make-up of the ruling class of the empire. At the same time, 30,000 Iranian youths who had been undergoing a Macedonian military training arrived in Susa. Alexander began to refer to them as his 'Successors'. The rise to prominence of these two groups makes it clear that Alexander was no longer thinking of his kingdom as a Macedonian one. Persians, suitably trained, were to play an important role. At the same time, there were to be no risks taken by placing Persians in positions of command; there, Macedonian men would take control.

Sir William Tarn built on these remarkable events a theory that Alexander originated, and believed in, an idea of 'the brotherhood of man' or 'unity of mankind', which we know to have been developed later by the Stoic philosopher Zeno and his successors, and which certainly influenced Plutarch's view of Alexander (Plut. *de fort. Alex.* 329 ff.). Tarn's idea became extremely influential, but was decisively demolished by Ernst Badian (1958), whose arguments repay reading in full. Tarn produced as direct evidence only one sentence from Arrian (Arr. *Anab.* 7.11.8–9) describing the banquet held at Opis a few weeks after the marriages. Alexander

> seated all the Macedonians round him, and next to them Persians, and then any persons from the other peoples who took precedence for rank or any other high quality, and he himself and those around him drank from the same bowl and poured the same libations, with the Greek soothsayers and Magi initiating the ceremony. Alexander prayed for various blessings and especially that the Macedonians and Persians should *enjoy harmony as partners in the government.*

This prayer is a very different thing from a philosophical belief in the unity of mankind as having one Father, Zeus, which is how Tarn represents the position. Indeed, it seems to represent rather clearly the position as established by the weddings, that Macedonians and Persians should work together to rule the empire. There is no mention of other peoples being involved.

A somewhat different view from Tarn's was developed by Ehrenberg (1938), who saw this 'policy' of 'fusion' as a development of Alexander's task of Hellenising the world. In fact, fusion and Hellenisation would seem to be at odds. Ehrenberg gave some consideration to the possible influence of Aristotle on Alexander's actions. But the one piece of advice we know Aristotle to have given Alexander was to treat the barbarians as slaves to the Greeks (fr 658 Rose) – precisely the opposite of what Alexander did here. We do not know what was contained in Aristotle's work 'On kingship' or in 'To Alexander on behalf of [or: concerning] the colonies'. It would seem surprisingly late in the day for Alexander suddenly to begin applying Aristotelian doctrines to his actions: he had not seen the man for more than ten years, though perhaps he had corresponded with him. It is much more satisfactory to interpret the strange and extravagant marriages as a pragmatic action, designed – though it failed – to ensure a reliable ruling class for the empire.

While the court was still at Susa, plans began to be laid for a further expedition by sea down the Arabian Gulf and the conquest of Arabia. But Babylon was now Alexander's immediate destination, for it was from there that that expedition was

to be launched. Babylon, where his treasure lay, was the effect-
ive centre of the empire. The next stage of the march brought
the court to Opis, on the bend of the Tigris close to the site of
modern Baghdad. Here the affairs of mainland Greece obtruded
themselves again as he addressed the question of superannuated
veterans.

The order of events is unclear, but the following seems the
most logical. In the summer of 324, Alexander announced the
dismissal, with generous severance pay, of some 10,000 veterans
who had served out their time. The soldiers were aggrieved at
what they saw as contempt for their achievements, and a near-
riot broke out in which the men challenged him to dismiss the
lot of them and continue his campaigning alone 'with his father
Ammon'. Alexander was enraged; he sent his officers among the
crowd, and thirteen ringleaders were arrested and dragged off
to instant execution. He then, according to Arrian, addressed
the stunned assembly in a speech which listed all the benefits the
Macedonians had received from himself 'and his father Philip',
who 'gave you cloaks to wear in place of skins . . . brought
you down from the mountains to the plains . . . made you
dwellers in cities and graced your lives with good laws and
customs' (Arr. *Anab.* 7.9.2; cf. Chapter 2 above). He pointed
out that the Macedonians remained the ruling élite of the
empire, that they had gained enormous wealth from the expedition, and that he himself had participated in all their many
dangers. He then retired to his tent for one of his heroic sulks.

He followed this by creating, as it were in pique, a number of
new Persian military units with Macedonian names, and appointed a number of Persian commanders to replace Macedonian ones. The Persians were entitled to be called his kinsmen and
to give and receive the king's kiss. The Macedonians, now
thoroughly cowed, gave way and complained that they were
never allowed to kiss the king. And so Alexander arranged the
banquet, mentioned above, at which Greeks, Persians and others
sat together in a show of unity. His crisis over the demobil-
isation was surmounted. Craterus was dispatched to lead the
veterans back to Greece and – a remarkable additional item –
to remove Antipater from his command as viceroy and take over
the rule of Macedon himself.

This sequence of events has several points of interest. First,
the taunting of Alexander as 'son of Ammon' raises the question

of his alleged desire to be regarded as a god, which will be discussed shortly. Second, the abrupt intention to replace the viceroy Antipater, who had been keeping Greece under control on Alexander's behalf for the last twelve years, cannot have been well received in Macedon, and it is not surprising that rumours arose after Alexander's death that Antipater had had a hand in it, as a way of forestalling his dismissal.

The immediate point of interest is the return of another 10,000 veterans to Greece. Already, in Carmania, Alexander, anxious to prevent further satrapal unrest, had ordered the dismissal of all mercenaries from the satrapal armies. In addition, the establishment by Antipater of puppet regimes in the Greek cities had resulted in the exile of many opponents. Alexander's strong-arm tactics had a disastrous effect which has been admirably summed up by Badian (1961,30):

> By his own actions – the policies that led to the reign of terror; the decision on mercenaries in the Persian service; the maintenance of puppet regimes in Greece; and finally the dissolution of the satrapal armies – the King had created an unprecedented and apparently insoluble social problem, which now turned out to be an unprecedented political and military problem as well: a mass of men with nothing to lose, and with military skill and training of the highest order, had suddenly been provided with leaders willing and able to use it. Nowhere in the short history of Alexander's reign does his ultimate political failure appear so nakedly as in the spiral of terrorism and fear that culminated in the situation of 324 BC.

Alexander's response to this situation was the promulgation of the Exiles Decree. This was pronounced at the Olympic Games (late July–early August) of 324, at which 20,000 of these exiles were present to hear it read. According to Diodorus, the only author to quote its wording, it ran as follows:

> King Alexander to the exiles from the Greek cities. We have not been the cause of your exile, but, save for those of you who are under a curse, we shall be the cause of your return to your native cities. We have written to Antipater about this to the end that if any cities are not willing to restore you, he may constrain them. (Diod. Sic. 18.8.4)

This decree was bound to cause social and political turmoil in the cities, and many of them were placed in a very difficult position by it. A large number of lawsuits and feuds inevitably ensued. In the circumstances it is not surprising that Athens was unwilling to negotiate with the suspect Harpalus: the arrival of this defector from Alexander's government must have seemed to expose them to punitive measures.

The most problematic point about this decree is the interpretation of its legal basis. Alexander was not king of Greece; the free cities were not part of his empire. He had no political authority to issue such a decree. How, then, was it to be enforced? The solution he chose was the simultaneous demand to the Greek cities that they proceed to offer him worship as a god. This demand was also promulgated at the Olympic Games, and led to several ironic *bon mots* from Greek statesmen. Damis the Spartan said, 'Well, let him be a god if he wants to.' Demosthenes in Athens finally conceded that Alexander could, for all he cared, become the son of Zeus – and of Poseidon, too, if he wanted. The Athenian orator Hypereides (*Epitaph*.21) complained, less humorously, that the Greeks were being compelled to honour rulers as gods and their servants as heroes. This is certainly a reference to Alexander and Hephaestion. (The complaint was remembered, and when Hypereides was captured after Athens rose against Macedon on Alexander's death Antipater had him executed, but only after his tongue had been cut out.)

The jokes concealed the remarkable change in political life that this decree introduced. Hitherto no man had become a god in his lifetime, though two dubious cases have been adduced: the Spartan general Lysander had received some kind of divine cult on Samos in the early fourth century, and Dion of Syracuse a little later may have been worshipped as a god in Syracuse. After Alexander, it became practically routine for the Hellenistic kings to adopt divine honours. The Roman emperors took up the practice. After Julius Caesar was posthumously deified by Augustus, Augustus himself found it expedient to accept cult as a god in the Greek East during his lifetime. The phenomenon has been brilliantly interpreted by Simon Price (1984) as something more than a mere political statement; in the free cities of Greece, the only way that an imperial ruler could lay claim to any authority over their lives was by adopting the supra-human status of a god. And in truth an emperor's power and status were above those of any individual king or city council. The same explanation may well be adopted for this move by Alexander (cf. Tarn 1948, II.370). Certainly people now behaved as if he were a god. Arrian (Arr. *Anab.* 7.23.2) says that the embassies at Babylon came to Alexander *hos theoroi dethen* – 'as if in the manner of sacred envoys'. The force of *dethen* here is ambiguous: it could mean that the envoys believed themselves to be on a sacred mission, or it could mean that they behaved – to the view of outsiders – as if they were on an embassy to a god. The linguistic arguments could pull either way, but I incline to the latter interpretation: the envoys did not actually believe that Alexander was a god, but observers were struck by their sanctimonious and grovelling behaviour.

This interpretation of events in effect sidesteps any question of whether Alexander actually believed in his own divinity. None the less, this question requires some consideration. There are degrees in Alexander's possible divinity. First, that he might be the son of a god. Callisthenes seems to have been the first to make much of the idea that Alexander was son of Zeus. Alexander, however, consistently refused to be so addressed. (The only exception is in Plutarch *Alex* 33, which is explicitly derived from Callisthenes, where Alexander encourages the Thessalians by referring in Homeric fashion to his descent from Zeus, and which is surely unhistorical.) However, as we have seen (Chapter 5), Alexander probably did regard himself as the son of the god Ammon. A hero might, of course, like Heracles, be the son of a god as well as of a mortal father, and might, in addition, become a god in his own right after his death.

The arguments that Alexander believed himself to be a god in his own right, already, are all connected with his relationship to Ammon. First, as pharaoh, he was certainly a god in Egypt. Even if he was never formally crowned, he was acknowledged as such and portrayed as pharaoh on temple reliefs. Second, as he accepted the orders of the oracle of Ammon that Hephaestion be worshipped as a hero only, he must have believed that Ammon had already sanctioned his own status as a god, or he could not in good faith have accepted the divine honours offered to himself (Badian 1981). Alexander's psychology at this stage of his career is impenetrable, but it seems highly likely that he did now believe in his own divinity. And he did indeed receive

cult in Athens and in some cities of Asia Minor in the last years
of his life.

A final curious piece of evidence in the case comes in a passage
of Aristotle's *Politics* (1286a 30 ff.), where he is discussing the
qualities of 'the good king':

> One would say it is impossible for such a one to divert or be
> changeable. One could not even rule over such a one, for that
> would be like ruling over Zeus himself. . . . The only thing
> remaining is that which appears actually to happen, that
> everyone should obey such a one willingly.

This passage was thought by Tarn to be a direct reference to
Alexander. He based his argument mainly on the change to the
singular 'such a one' from the plurals in the preceding sentences.
It has to be said that the argument is tenuous, and the dismissal
of it by Ehrenberg, despite Tarn's subsequent defence, remains
cogent. However, it would be evidence only for Aristotle's ideas
about Alexander, not for Alexander's own.

The last important event of the summer of 324 took place
after the court had removed from Opis to the cooler climate of
Ecbatana (Hamadan) in the Zagros mountains. Here a lavish
festival was staged, with deep drinking every evening. During
these festivities, Alexander's close friend Hephaestion fell ill and
died. Arrian tells us only that his illness lasted seven days. The
other sources are equally brief, and the relevant portion of
Curtius is lost. Our only further information about his death
comes from some quotations from a lost work by Ephippus
entitled *The Deaths of Alexander and Hephaestion*. All these are
preserved in one work, the *Deipnosophists* of Athenaeus, an
author whose interest lay in eating and drinking habits, and
whose inclination was to censure excess and luxury in their
application. So it is no surprise to find that the passages of
Ephippus he quotes attribute the death of Hephaestion and of
Alexander to their excessive drinking. Plutarch simply tells us
that he developed a fever, and disobeyed his doctor's instructions by eating a whole boiled fowl and a huge amount of
wine. He died shortly afterwards.

Alexander's grief was on a heroic scale. An Achilles to
Hephaestion's Patroclus, the prostrate king mourned his friend
for a day and a night. Even Arrian is prepared to accept that
Alexander 'probably' cut off his hair over the corpse, though he

rejects the report that he had the temple of Asclepius (the god of healing) at Ecbatana razed to the ground, and does not even mention the story (which is in Plutarch) that he had Hephaestion's doctor crucified. The body was embalmed and sent ahead to Babylon, where the following spring it was to be burned on a magnificent pyre that cost 10,000 talents to prepare. According to Diodorus' description (Diod. Sic. 17.115.1–5), it covered an area some 600 by 200 metres.

> Upon the foundation course were golden prows of quinque-remes in close order ... each carried two kneeling archers four cubits in height and (on the deck) armed male figures five cubits high, while the intervening spaces were occupied by red banners fashioned out of felt.

The second level held torches fifteen cubits high; the third a carved scene of a hunt; the fourth a centauromachy in gold; and the fifth a frieze of lions and bulls, also in gold. Above these was a layer of Macedonian and Persian weaponry, and

> on top of all stood Sirens, hollowed out and able to conceal within them persons who sang a lament in mourning for the dead. The total height of the pyre was more than one hundred and thirty cubits.

It should be remarked that this structure was probably never completed, even though Diodorus writes as if it was. Its completion was part of the 'Last Plans' rejected by the Macedonian assembly after Alexander's death (see below). In preparation for all this magnificence, Alexander, as mentioned above, sent messengers to the oracle of Ammon at Siwa, to enquire whether it was proper that Hephaestion should be worshipped as a god. The answer that came back in the spring of 323 is variously given. Arrian (Arr. *Anab.* 7.23.6) says 'they reported that Ammon said that it was lawful to sacrifice to Hephaestion as a hero' (so also Plutarch). Diodorus, however (Diod. Sic. 17.115.6), says that the response permitted him to be worshipped as a god. Justin agrees with this, and Lucian in his work on *On Not Believing Slander Readily* says that temples were erected to him, oaths sworn by him, and divine sacrifices offered. These claims must be treated with scepticism, but Alexander may have encouraged their development. We know that his governor in Egypt, Cleomenes, who was a corrupt administrator, earned Alexander's explicit pardon for his acts by having hero-shrines built for Hephaestion and instituting his name as a guarantee in the preamble of mercantile contracts. This may be what Lucian has in mind. Arrian disapproves strongly of this readiness in Alexander to forgive corruption when the perpetrator favoured his own predilections.

The winter of 324/3 was spent in reducing an Iranian hill tribe, the Cossaeans, and early in 323 the court set out for Babylon. At Babylon, Alexander was met by embassies from several parts of the world. The Libyans sent crowns, and other peoples who came included Celts, Iberians, Scythians and Ethiopians. Several Italian peoples – Bruttians, Etruscans and Lucanians – also sent representatives, though it is certainly fantasy, as Arrian insists, that includes ambassadors from Rome among their number. Even the Carthaginians are supposed to have sent envoys. The purposes of these missions are unclear and were probably various. The Greek cities sent greetings and presumably wished to be known to be complying with his decree of the previous summer. Whether divine honours were also offered is not clear (see above). The other peoples, it seems likely, had become aware that Alexander had finished conquering the east, and wished to forestall a military onslaught against their own lands. It is significant that no embassy arrived from the Arabians; Alexander seems to have interpreted this absence as a good reason to press on with his plans for a military expedition to Arabia. The army was remodelled again, with the incorporation of large numbers of Persian infantry into the Macedonian phalanx, and the fleet began to undertake exercises in anticipation of the departure.

The emperor Augustus is said to have marvelled at Alexander's unwillingness, having conquered a vast empire, to do anything at all to set it in order (Plutarch, *Sayings of Kings and Commanders* 207D8). In fact Alexander was bored. He wanted to be on the move again. In addition, he was anxious to be out of Babylon, for before he arrived there he had received a number of dispiriting prophecies from the Chaldaean priests in Babylon. He had complied with their insistence that he enter the city not from the west (the natural direction) but from the east, which had entailed following a difficult and circuitous route. Ill-omened sacrifices by the Greek priests added to his disquiet, and he remembered the remark of Calanus as he ascended his pyre that he would meet Alexander again at Babylon (that is, in death). Curious portents also took place during his stay at Babylon. On one occasion, a Babylonian prisoner broke loose and ascended Alexander's throne, calmly seating himself on it and placing the diadem on his head. On another, Alexander was sailing on the Tigris when his sunhat flew off; a sailor dived in to fetch it and brought it back safe by the expedient of placing it on his own head as he swam. The first story may, it is suggested by Peter Green, have something to do with a Babylonian ritual of the Mock King, connected with the New Year festival; however that may be, both acts constituted *lèse majesté*, and the sailor received not only a reward but also a flogging for his ill-omened action. Arrian says that most historians say Alexander actually had the man beheaded, Aristobulus being the authority for the more moderate version. A later elaboration turned the sailor into the future king Seleucus, his claim to royalty established by this omen (App. *Syr.* 52 ff.; Fraser 1996, 36–7). The *Alexander Romance* (3.30) adds a different story of a monstrous birth of a half-human, half-animal child, of which only the animal half showed signs of life, which was interpreted by the Chaldaeans as an omen of the death of the king.

On 29 May, soon after the return of the messengers from Siwa, a banquet was held. In the middle of this Alexander was taken ill and retired to bed. His fever increased as the days went by, despite frequent bathing, sacrifices, and rest under a canopy by the river. After some days the army insisted on filing past his sickbed to say their farewells. Several of Alexander's officers slept in the temple of Sarapis (the process known as incubation), seeking to learn by a dream vision whether it would be better for Alexander to be brought into the temple, but received the reply that it would be better for him to stay where he was. Shortly after this, on 10 June 323, Alexander died.

Arrian quotes as his authority for this sequence of events, including the file-past and the incubation in the temple, the 'Royal Journal'. Dispute has raged over the authenticity of this document, which has not survived; a commentary was written on it in the third century by Strattis of Olynthus, but this is also lost. Most recent scholars, following Lionel Pearson, have supposed it to be a later forgery, and have pointed chiefly to the mention in this episode of Sarapis, a god whose worship was not established until the reign of Ptolemy I in Alexandria, and who is quite unlikely to have had a shrine in Babylon, as proof that the 'Journal' was a later composition. (Strattis has also been impugned as a forgery by some scholars.) There is no certain indication that the 'Journal' covered any period before June 324. N. G. L. Hammond (1983, 1988 and 1993), however, returning to the view of Wilcken, has argued strongly that the 'Royal Journal' was a genuine document covering the whole reign of Alexander; that such journals were kept for all Macedonian kings; that it was the fundamental source for the detailed histories of both Ptolemy and Aristobulus; and that to forge a document of such length, when the original was extant, would be a pointless exercise which would never win credence. Eumenes, as royal secretary, would have been the author of this official journal. Hammond's arguments have not won acceptance. Bosworth (1971b) proposes a new solution, suggesting that the document is genuine – by the hand of Eumenes – but not official. He argues that the reference to Sarapis could not be in a later forged document, as by that time the Sarapis cult was so developed that an assimilation to the Babylonian Bel-Marduk would be impossible, whereas at an earlier date Sarapis might have been used as a Greek equivalent for the Babylonian god. He suggests that the document is part of the propaganda war associated with the days immediately after Alexander's death, designed to counter any suspicions of poisoning. The work of Eumenes (whose further career was linked to the regent Perdiccas) would thus be a tool to enhance the claims of those who did inherit Alexander's authority. This is a subtle and attractive explanation, but as with so many crucial issues a definitive answer is unlikely ever to emerge.

At any rate, Arrian's is the most sober account we have of Alexander's death. The question of the cause of Alexander's death has naturally exercised historians from the moment of its occurrence. The implication of the story is that, as with Hephaestion, excessive drinking of wine was the primary cause. An equally likely possibility is that Alexander had succumbed to malaria in the Tigris marshes (as Hephaestion might also have done during the stay at Opis). His constitution was indubitably weakened by his numerous wounds and hard campaigning. The *accidie* he felt in Babylon may also have been a sign of disease.

But it was perhaps inevitable that his death should soon be attributed to the effects of poison. This story, which is mentioned in all the sources (e.g. Curt. 10.10.14), is elaborated in the *Alexander Romance*, and further developed in the *Liber de Morte Alexandri* (a Latin work no earlier than the fourth century AD, but using earlier sources: Heckel 1988). In this version, Antipater was the culprit; he was afraid of Alexander and hated Olympias, and seized an opportunity to get rid of him. He sent the poison by the hand of his son Cassander, who had led the Greek embassy to Babylon a short while previously, and had experienced a quite terrifying first meeting with the king, so that ever afterwards he could never see a statue of him without breaking out into shivers. The poison was said to have been administered by Iollas, Cassander's brother, as cupbearer. According to the *Alexander Romance*, Alexander was in such pain that he made to throw himself into the river to end it all, and was only rescued by Roxane who came running after him. Both these details are alluded to by Arrian, and the poisoning story in general is discussed by all the historians (though in Curtius the actual narrative of the death has been lost). Diodorus states that this version only became current after the death of Cassander in 287; it perhaps arose with Hieronymus of Cardia, whose history went from the death of Alexander to about 263 BC. In 317 BC, Olympias, having helped Polyperchon to wrest control of Macedonia from Cassander, put to death Cassander's brother Nicanor, and overturned the tomb of Iollas, on the pretext of avenging the death of Alexander (Diod. Sic. 19.11.8). But that is the extent of the evidence for the poisoning, and it is on balance more likely that Alexander's death was from natural causes.

His death created enormous problems. His empire began to fall apart immediately. A revolt of the Greek colonists in Bactria led to the establishment of an independent kingdom there. The Greeks instantly revolted against Antipater: their rising led to the Lamian War which lasted throughout the winter of 323/2. The great problem was that of the succession. Alexander had died without an heir, though Roxane was pregnant and pro-duced a child in August 323. He was named Alexander IV and created co-regent with Alexander's mentally defective half-brother Philip III Arrhidaeus; but it is obvious that power lay elsewhere. Alexander had failed to make any provisions for the succession, and his dying words were singularly unhelpful.

When he, at length, despaired of life, he took off his ring and handed it to Perdiccas [who in effect had succeeded Hephaestion as second-in-command]. His Friends asked 'To whom do you leave the kingdom?' and he replied 'To the strongest'. He added, and these were his last words, that all of his leading Friends would stage a vast contest in honour of his funeral. (Diod. Sic. 18.117.4)

In practice Perdiccas assumed command in Babylon, and Antipater in Macedonia. Craterus also had some obscure role in Macedonia (though he did not oust Antipater) but died in 321. Perdiccas executed some thirty Macedonians who opposed his position, as well as one Meleager, who had staged an attempted coup in favour of Arrhidaeus, and sent Pithon to quell the Bactrian rebels. Eumenes, the king's secretary (a Greek), who had control of the state papers, threw in his lot with Perdiccas. The latter became guardian of the kings, later ceding this position to Polyperchon. In 317, Arrhidaeus' wife challenged Polyperchon; she and her husband were soon dead. Cassander succeeded to Antipater's rule in Macedon. Ptolemy made himself master of Egypt and repelled an invasion (321) of Perdiccas, who was killed in the campaign. A temporary settlement between the rival factions at Triparadeisus in 320 did not last. Antigonus, the satrap of Asia Minor, made himself master of Asia, which by 306 had been split up, leaving him the land west of the Euphrates (except Thrace, which went to Lysimachus), while the eastern satrapies became the kingdom of Seleucus. The wars of the Successors were in theory concluded by the battle of Ipsus in 301, but the world empire was never brought together again.

These events provide the context for several problematic documents which circulated soon after Alexander's death, notably his 'Will' and his 'Last Plans'. The Will is preserved in the *Alexander Romance* (3.32). It is presented as addressed to the people of Rhodes, and this betrays its origin as a piece of propaganda bolstering the Rhodians' case after their expulsion of the Macedonian garrison following the death of Alexander. But it also contains much more detail about the division of the empire among the various commanders – Craterus in Macedon, Ptolemy in Egypt, Perdiccas and Antigonus in Asia, Lysimachus in Thrace, as well as dispositions in the eastern satrapies and the appointment of Arrhidaeus as co-king with Roxane's child, if male. A surprising detail is the allocation of Illyria to Holkias. A subtle analysis of this document by Waldemar Heckel (1988) has concluded that it originated in the circle of Polyperchon, and generally favours the Perdiccan grouping with which Polyperchon was allied. The otherwise obscure Holkias, it has been conjectured, may be the author of the 'Will'.

Larger questions are raised by the 'Last Plans' of Alexander.

> Craterus . . . had received written instructions which the king had given him for execution; nevertheless, after the death of Alexander, it seemed best to the successors not to carry out these plans. (Diod. Sic. 18.4.1)

The first item was the completion of the pyre of Hephaestion; but the memorandum then, allegedly, went on to propose the building of 1000 warships for a campaign against Carthage; the building of a road along the Libyan coast as far as the Pillars of Hercules (Straits of Gibraltar); the erection of temples at Delos, Delphi, Dodona and Ilium, and at Dium, Amphipolis and Cyrnus in Macedonia; and the establishment of numerous cities and the transplantation of 'populations from Asia to Europe and in the opposite direction from Europe to Asia, in order to bring the largest contingents to a common unity and to friendly kinship by means of intermarriages and family ties' (Diod. Sic. 18.4.5). A tomb was to be built for Philip to match the Pyramids of Egypt.

W. W. Tarn rejected these 'Plans' as a forgery, except for the temple at Ilium and Hephaestion's pyre, which are independently reported. More recent scholars, notably Schachermeyr, Badian and Bosworth, in a return to the view of Wilcken, have argued for the acceptance of these 'Last Plans' as a genuine memorandum of Alexander's. None of the proposals seems utterly implausible as an expression of Alexander's psychology in his last days.

A major point, the transportation of peoples, was used in the last century by German scholars to support the idea that Alexander dreamed of world conquest. Tarn, despite his belief that Alexander had an idea of the Brotherhood of Man, rejected this corollary of his belief. However, it is possible to imagine that such ideas were at least consonant with Alexander's own ambitions, and there were Assyrian and Persian precedents for the procedure. The other points may be distorted but need not be rejected. Tarn's argument that Alexander could not have thought of building a military road because the Romans were the first to build such roads is a particularly weak one, and a campaign to the Pillars of Hercules and beyond would fit with ambitions for world-conquest.

The question that arises, if the 'Plans' are genuine, is how they were presented. Tarn thought that Diodorus had confused a forged document prepared by Perdiccas to ensure that the 'Plans' were voted down with the actual, more limited orders, given to Craterus in respect of his arrival in Macedonia. Badian, however, suggests that Perdiccas, besides wanting these grandiose plans annulled, also wanted to stop Craterus from reaching Macedonia: accordingly he included the orders to Craterus in the plans he presented to the assembly for rejection.

The 'Last Plans', then, tell us something about Alexander's ambitions; but the way they were presented by Perdiccas tells us more about the struggle for power following Alexander's death.

We may conclude the story with the temporary appropriation of Alexander's power by Perdiccas, and the abandonment of Alexander's further ambitions for world conquest. The Macedonian Empire had entered a new, fissiparous phase.

Alexander's body itself became an immediate object of rivalry and symbol of power. An immense catafalque was prepared, which began to trundle its way slowly across Asia to bring the embalmed body to the burial-place of the Macedonian kings at Aegae. (Curtius, 10.5.4, says that Alexander expressed a dying wish to be buried at Siwa, but this was not to happen.) It was soon hijacked by Ptolemy, already establishing his power in Egypt, and redirected to Memphis. Eventually it ended up in Alexandria. Roman emperors visited his tomb there as Alexander had visited Achilles' at Troy. As the prophecy of Sarapis in the *Romance* 'foretold' (1.33).

> You shall live in it
> For all time, dead and yet not dead.
> The city you have built shall be your tomb.

9

Conclusion

This book began by suggesting that Alexander's career was the motive force for the spread of Hellenism throughout the western Mediterranean and the Near East, and that his achievement thus provided the matrix in which the Roman Empire, Christianity and other important aspects of western civilisation could take root. The narrative and analysis carried out in the course of the book will, I hope, have shown that such grandiose prospects were far from Alexander's imagining and that his own aims and ambitions were very different. It is time to draw some of the threads together and to bring those aims and ambitions face-to-face with his actual legacy.

The preceding chapter considered Alexander's 'Last Plans'. On the assumption, current today among most scholars, that they represent genuine plans of Alexander, we can deduce that Alexander's megalomania was increasing. He had come to believe, in some degree, his own propaganda, that made him a son of the god Ammon and possibly divine himself. Buttressed by this sublime form of self-confidence (and he had never, at any stage of his career, been short of confidence), he had become increasingly ruthless in executing his purposes. Disloyalty was instantly punished, but corruption and peculation were treated with casualness as long as the perpetrator's loyalty was not in doubt. Opportunistic and flexible, Alexander had been as quick to lose his conquests in India as he had been to gain them, abandoning them when they no longer threatened his immediate position. Babylon and Iran had become the heartland of his empire, but what kind of empire was that to be?

Administration was never to his taste, and Augustus' observation that Alexander had done surprisingly little to set in order the vast empire he had gained is a telling one. The king's state of mind seems to have been a strange one in his last months; besides his megalomania, he was perhaps already ill with the disease that killed him and suffering from a consequent *accidie*. The only activity he could conceive of that was worthy of his self-image was further conquest. Preparations were already far advanced for the invasion of Arabia, and it is not unreasonable to believe that he had plans to conquer the west – Italy and Carthage, and perhaps beyond. Italians and Carthaginians plainly believed it.

In hindsight it may seem inevitable that an empire based purely on rapid military conquest could not be held together. It was Alexander's pleasure to have his satraps loyal to him; he was not interested in imposing a uniform style of government on his empire, and the Greek lands were virtually forgotten. It was inevitable that such an empire would collapse once his own strong personality was removed. In addition, the fact that he did nothing to appoint a successor strengthened this inevitability. It seems even that he may have revelled in the idea that his death would lead to dissolution of his work: witness his remark that his successors would stage an immense funeral contest over his body, and his alleged dying bequest of his kingdom 'to the strongest'. The confusing years of the wars of the Successors, down to the battle of Ipsus in 301, and the subsequent development of several very distinct Hellenistic monarchies, lead into a very different world from that of the adventurer.

But it was a world that spoke Greek. In addition, all the successor kings revered the memory of Alexander as their founder. All minted coins with his image. Around Seleucus a legend (a 'Seleucus-romance', in P. M. Fraser's (1996.36) expression) grew up which cast Seleucus as the divinely designated successor to Alexander: for it had been he who had swum to retrieve the diadem which had blown from Alexander's head, and had placed it on his own. Ptolemy in Egypt had the advantage of having Alexander's body at hand as legitimating token of his authority.

Macedon is often overlooked in the context of these vaster empires. Let us look first at the legacy he left to his own land. In a provocative article entitled 'Alexander the Great and the decline of Macedon', Bosworth (1986) has drawn attention to the disastrous effect of Alexander's conquests on Macedonian manpower. In addition to the initial expeditionary force, consisting predominantly of Macedonians, there were several waves of reinforcements, so that before the events at Opis there were still 18,000 Macedonians among the infantry – more than the original expedition. Bosworth calculates that probably as many as 40,000 men joined Alexander's army from Macedon in the eleven years of his expedition. Many were killed; more were settled in colonies as distant as Bactria; few ever returned home. It is inevitable that the population must have declined; and in the circumstances it is not surprising that Alexander organised Macedonian training for large numbers of Persian youths. This was not a mixing of cultures, but simply an attempt to produce a sufficiency of fighting men of the kind he needed. Nothing could indicate more clearly the essentially pragmatic – not to say ruthless – springs of Alexander's actions. Macedon was neglected to feed his own ambition. He left to his heirs a greatly weakened kingdom, so that it is truly remarkable that Macedon was able to become again a significant military power in the Mediterranean before its final crushing by the Roman military machine in the early second century BC.

If we turn now from Macedon to the wider world, we can see that, although it was far from Alexander's intention to mingle cultures for any kind of altruistic or philosophical motive, it was an end result of his actions that the cultures did mix. This happened at different rates, and in different degrees, in different parts of the empire. Greece, with its strong cultural traditions, was essentially unaffected by the empire. The city-states continued their own way under Macedonian overlordship, though they had to get used to honouring 'Royal Friends'. The same is largely true of the Greek cities of Asia Minor, which were able to continue as 'independent cities' under the relatively weak rule of Antigonus and then Lysimachus. Some of the cities prospered remarkably, notably Pergamon which developed a literary and artistic culture to rival that of Alexandria itself. When the last Attalid king of Pergamon bequeathed his kingdom to Rome, the fate of the rest of Asia Minor was also sealed.

Further to the east, the Seleucid kingdom which came to centre on Syria proved relatively long-lasting, despite constant territorial wars with Ptolemaic Egypt in which Judaea-Palestine in particular was shuttled between the two kingdoms. Seleucus inherited most of the Iranian territories but made more impact on the lands west of the Euphrates, founding many cities, often in his own name (as Seleuceia) or in that of members of his family (Apamea) or of Macedonian cities (Edessa, Europus, Berrhoea); but he probably named a good many of his cities Alexandria, thus providing a source of confusion for later historians who have taken these to be Alexander's own foundations.

Ptolemy's Egypt was the most illustrious and long-lasting of the successor kingdoms, maintaining an unbroken dynasty until the conquest by Augustus of Antony and Cleopatra (the last Ptolemaic queen) in 31 BC. Alexandria, largely as a result of the cultural patronage of Ptolemy II, became a centre of literature and the arts. The Library at Alexandria was the greatest in the world and supported a huge staff of scholar-librarians who were also the focus of a literary renaissance. Jewish literature also flourished in Alexandria; the Jewish scriptures were translated into Greek, and many other Jewish authors, based in Egypt, wrote works of history, philosophy or poetry in Greek. This represented the first genuine cross-fertilisation of cultures resulting from Alexander's conquests (though Greeks were less ready to hear from Jews than Jews from Greeks). The Egyptian historian Manetho also wrote in Greek, as did the Babylonian historian Berossus. As we shall see, the *Alexander Romance*, which carried the Alexander legend into the Middle Ages, was plainly written in Alexandria.

A less long-lived but perhaps even more dramatic legacy of Alexander's conquests was the Greek kingdom of Bactria. The tribal society of Bactria suffered more upheaval as a result of the conquest than any other part of the empire. Several cities were founded in the region, and military garrisons were stationed to form a governing élite; native princes and satraps were left with relatively little power. Not all the Greeks and Macedonians liked it in Bactria; on receiving the news of Alexander's death, one large group decided to up sticks and return to the homeland. They had to be dissuaded by Perdiccas; the method he used was massacre. Those that remained developed a Greek civilisation of their own.

The history of the kingdom of Bactria which broke loose from Seleucid rule in the mid-third century is known only from scattered references and from its magnificent coinage. Its mineral resources enabled it to prosper under King Diodotus and his successors, who extended fingers of control deeper into Central Asia and as far as Ferghana. In about 187, King Demetrius, modelling himself on Alexander, conducted an invasion of India. The most glorious of the Bactrian kings was Menander (mid-second century) who ruled parts of northern India and was a considerable patron of culture, too. An important relic of this period is the long Buddhist instructional work, the *Questions of King Milinda*. Milinda is the Greek king Menander, and the work consists of questions put by him to a sage, whose answers constitute a complete conspectus of Buddhist teaching.

In time Greek style merged with the native traditions of Buddhism to produce a remarkable flowering in the form of the religious art of Gandhara. Here, for the first time, the stories of the Buddha, and the various meditative postures of the Lord, were portrayed in sculpture; and the style is heavily indebted to the humanistic, naturalistic style of classical Greek art. Proportion, posture, expression – all are clearly Greek despite the adaptation to the different physiognomies of north-west India. There is no doubt that Greek, or Greek-trained, artists produced this, the most visible witness of the impact of Greek civilisation on the subcontinent.

The kingdom died out in the mid-first century AD, but it put down roots sufficiently deep for princes in the nineteenth century proudly to claim descent from Alexander the Great. (These beliefs are the mainspring of Kipling's powerful story, 'The Man Who Would Be King', about a British soldier who passes himself off to the natives as the reincarnation of Alexander.)

Finally we must turn to the philosophical and literary impact of Alexander. Mention has already been made of the work of Onesicritus and the associated developments of the story of Alexander's encounter with the 'naked philosophers' at Taxila. This story embedded Alexander firmly in the Cynic philosophical tradition. In this story Alexander became a somewhat sympathetic figure, a seeker after truth and simplicity; whereas in the other great Cynic story about Alexander, that of his meeting with Diogenes, the 'founder' of the Cynic school, he is portrayed as an incorrigible tyrant.

Other philosophical schools also took an interest in Alexander as an *exemplum*. It used to be thought, mainly as a result of the work of Tarn, that there was an identifiable 'Peripatetic' view of Alexander, deriving from the hostile work of Callisthenes, the nephew of Aristotle the founder of the Peripatetics (so-called from the Peripatos where they 'walked about' – *peripatein* – while engaged in philosophical discussion). Later scholarship has shown that there was no such monolithic philosophical view of Alexander.

The Stoics, too (so called from the Stoa or portico in which they held their discussions), had an interest in Alexander. It surfaces mainly in the works of Roman writers such as Cicero and Seneca, who were drawing on now lost Greek works (in the case of Cicero, the polymath Posidonius, *c*.135–*c*.51 BC). Here, too, it is not possible to identify a single 'view' represented by these writers; but there is a considerable emphasis on Alexander as the tyrant, enslaved to his pride – and even his lust – and corrupted by good fortune. Hence Plutarch, who admired Alexander, wrote his two essays 'On the fortune of Alexander' to dispute such interpretations. It must be borne in mind that Arrian, the greatest and most authoritative of the Alexander historians, was himself a Stoic philosopher and the author of several philosophical works.

Such philosophical concerns with Alexander as an 'ideal' example of extreme behaviour kept his reputation alive throughout antiquity and into the Christian period. But alongside this philosophical hostility to Alexander, and his casting as a paragon of wickedness by some Christian writers, who largely developed the Stoic objections to his character, there was a second strand which might be regarded as a kind of hagiography. This was represented by the *Alexander Romance*, which was certainly written in Alexandria (because of its emphasis on the foundation legends of Alexandria) and is probably the work of less than a century after Alexander's death. It combined a number of existing Alexander traditions – an epistolary novel about his conquests, descriptions of the exotic lands he visited, documents from the propaganda war following his death, a list of his city foundations, and an ever expanding repertoire of wonder tales – to create a narrative which, constantly rewritten over the centuries (there are five quite distinct ancient Greek versions, not to speak of medieval and modern Greek ones, and four Latin ones) and translated into thirty-seven languages of both east and west (from Syriac, Armenian, Ethiopic and Hebrew – five versions – to Old Serbian, Icelandic and Irish), carried the name of Alexander to every culture of Europe and the Middle East. What is truly fascinating about the text is the way the figure of Alexander becomes Protean: he serves to emblematise the dominant concerns and anxieties of the host culture and to become a kind of Everyman for every author. In this way his reputation and influence have outlived even the very remarkable historical achievements which it has been the purpose of this book to summarise.

Bibliography

Badian, E. (1958), 'Alexander the Great and the unity of mankind', *Historia* 7:425–44.

Badian, E. (1960), 'The death of Parmenio' *TAPA* 91:324–38.

Badian, E. (1961), 'Harpalus', *JHS* 81:16–43.

Badian, E. (1965), 'The date of Clitarchus', *PACA* 8:5–11.

Badian, E. (1976), 'Some recent interpretations of Alexander', *Entretiens Hardt* 22:279–311.

Badian, E. (1981), 'The deification of Alexander the Great', in *Ancient Macedonian Studies in Honor of Charles F. Edson*, ed. H. Dell. Thessaloniki.

Badian, E. (1996), 'Alexander the Great between two thrones and Heaven: variations on an old theme', in *Subject and Ruler: Journal of Roman Archaeology Supplement No. 17*, ed. Alastair Small.

Bagnall, R. S. (1979), 'The date of the foundation of Alexandria', *AJAH* 4:46–9.

Borza, E. M. (1981), 'Anaxarchus and Callisthenes: academic intrigue at Alexander's court', in *Ancient Macedonian Studies in Honor of Charles F. Edson*, ed. H. Dell. Thessaloniki. Reprinted in Borza, *Makedonika*, ed. Carol G. Thomas. Claremont, Calif., 1995.

Bosworth, A. B. (1971a), 'Philip II and Upper Macedonia', *CQ* 21.93–105.

Bosworth, A. B. (1971b), 'The death of Alexander the Great: rumour and propaganda', *CQ* 21:112–36.

Bosworth, A. B. (1977), 'Alexander and Ammon', in *Greece and the Ancient Mediterranean in History and Prehistory: Studies Presented to Fritz Schachermeyr*, ed. K. Kinzl. Berlin.

Bosworth, A. B. (1986), 'Alexander the Great and the decline of Macedon', *JHS* 106:1–12.

Bosworth, A. B. (1988), *Conquest and Empire: The Reign of Alexander the Great*, Cambridge.

Brunt, A. B. (1976 and 1983), *Arrian: History of Alexander and Indica*, Loeb Classical Library, Vols I and II.

Cawkwell, G. L. (1978), *Philip of Macedon*.

Droysen, J. G. (1952), *Geschichte des Hellenismus I: Geschichte Alexanders des Grossen*, 2nd edn, Gotha, 1877; 3rd edn, Basel.

Ehrenberg, V. (1938), *Alexander and the Greeks*. Oxford.

Engels, D. W. (1978), *Alexander the Great and the Logistics of the Macedonian Army*. Berkeley, Calif.

Foss, C. (1977), 'The battle of the Granicus: a new look', *Ancient Macedonia* 2 (Thessaloniki), 495–502.

Fox, Robin Lane (1973), *Alexander the Great*. London.

Fraser, P. M. (1996), *Cities of Alexander the Great*. Oxford.

Green, Peter (1974), *Alexander of Macedon*. Harmondsworth; reissued Berkeley, Calif., 1991

Griffith, G. T. (1966) (ed.), *Alexander the Great: The Main Problems*. Cambridge.

Hamilton, J. R. (1969), *Plutarch: Alexander: a commentary*. Oxford.

Hamilton, J. R. (1971), 'Alexander and the Aral', *CQ* 21:106–11.

Hammond, N. G. L. (1983), *Three Historians of Alexander the Great*. Cambridge.

Hammond, N. G. L. (1988), 'The Royal Journals of Alexander the Great', *Historia* 37:129–50.

Hammond, N. G. L. (1993), *Sources for Alexander the Great*. Cambridge.

Heckel, Waldemar (1988), *The Last Days and Testament of Alexander the Great*. Stuttgart.

Heckel, Waldemar (1992), *The Marshals of Alexander's Empire*. London.

Pearson, Lionel (1960), *The Lost Histories of Alexander the Great*. New York.

Price, M. J. (1991), *The Coinage in the Names of Alexander the Great and Philip Arrhidaeus*, 2 vols. London.

Price, S. R. F. (1984), *Rituals and Power: The Roman Imperial Cult in Asia Minor*. Cambridge.

Robinson, C. A. (1953, 1963), *The History of Alexander the Great*, 2 vols. Providence, RI.

Schachermeyr, F. (1940), *Indogermanen und Orient*. Vienna.

Schachermeyr, F. (1973), *Alexander der Grosse: das Problem seiner Persönlichkeit und seines Wirkens*. Vienna.

Stein, Sir Aurel (1929), *On Alexander's Track to the Indus*. London.

Stewart, Andrew (1993), *Faces of Power: Alexander's Image and Hellenistic Politics*. Berkeley, Calif.

Stoneman, Richard (1991), *The Greek Alexander Romance*. Harmondsworth.

Stoneman, Richard (1994), *Legends of Alexander the Great*. London.

Stoneman, Richard (1995), 'Naked philosophers: the Brahmans in the Alexander historians and the *Alexander Romance*', *JHS* 115:99–114.

Tarn, W. W. (1948), *Alexander the Great*, I–II. Cambridge.

Welles, C. B. (1962), 'The discovery of Sarapis and the foundation of Alexandria', *Historia* 11:271–98.

Wilcken, Ulrich (1923), 'Alexander der Grosse und die indischen Gymnosophisten', *Sb. Akad. Berlin, ph.-hist. klasse*, 150–83.

Wilcken, Ulrich (1967), *Alexander the Great*, translated with introduction, notes and bibliography by E. N. Borza. New York. The original German edition was published in 1922.

Worthington, Ian (1984), 'The first flight of Harpalus reconsidered', *Greece and Rome* 31:161–9.